COME DOWN DARK PRINCE!

DICK BERNAL

Whitaker House

COME DOWN DARK PRINCE

ISBN: 0-88368-282-6
Printed in the United States of America
©1989 by Dick Bernal

Unless otherwise indicated, all Scripture quotations are taken from the *King James Version* of the Bible.

Whitaker House
580 Pittsburgh Street
Springdale, PA 15144

Introduction

GOD'S JUDGMENT ON NATIONS*

The foundations of present-day America are no longer solid rocks cemented in its Christian heritage. They have become brittle clay crumbling under the judgment of God.

The landscape of history is strewn with the remains of nations, once great, who let moral decay from within bring them to ruin.

As the Roman Empire rose to greatness, its populace no doubt assumed that it would be around for centuries to come. But even while its citizens romped in apparent prosperity, its foundations were crumbling underneath them. And so historians record "The Rise and the Fall of the Roman Empire."

Greece gave the world its first historical attempt at democracy, splendid architecture, excellence in culture. It produced a dazzling roster of men, including Socrates, Plato and Aristotle. Greek civilization rose to its "Golden Age," until corruption set in: in politics, business, personal life, even religion. According to a popular proverb, there were more gods in Athens than men! The Apostle Paul clearly identified that nation's spiritual poverty when from Mars Hill he preached his famous sermon on their "unknown God." In time Greece fell. And with it their democracy fell, because Greece did not have the moral fiber to undergird it.

Other great civilizations have come and gone. The ancient Mayan nation developed brain surgery, excelled in mathematics and astronomy, and built an incredible network of irrigation canals. Then corruption took hold. Today it is a ghost of the past.

*See tribute at end of Introduction.

America: Next on the List?

Is God blind to the sin of our own nation? Will He continue to bless us as He looks on our idols of silver and gold, on our pride of personal achievement, on our prevailing rebellion against Him?

The Bible repeatedly warns that, without repentance, judgment is inevitable. "Righteousness exalteth a nation; but sin is a reproach to any people."

America is not big enough to shake her fist in the face of a holy God and get away with it. Does the black shadow of judgment already loom over our land?

As America has permitted homosexuality to establish itself as an "alternate life-style," it has also reeled from the frightening spread of sexually transmitted diseases. Sin begets its own consequences, both on individuals and nations.

As it opened the doors to abortion, it found itself a party to wholesale murder and inherited a whole new set of social problems.

As it pulled the Judeo-Christian moral foundations from its schools, it invited an epidemic of drugs, rebellion and classroom assaults.

As it let its military respect slide, Communism added new pieces of geography to its campaign of world conquest, and millions more around the world lost their freedoms.

While the economy has seemingly rebounded, at least for the moment, some analysts still point to the darkening shadows of economic catastrophe. Stories of crime, corruption and sex scandal fill the newspapers. Conservatives and liberals alike agree that our beloved nation has some gaping wounds. Sadly, though, the combined attempts of analysts, politicians, educators and sociologists are failing miserably to provide any lasting solutions. Why? We have failed to understand the cause of our problems. As a result, we are merely treating symptoms, while ignoring the real roots.

The Root of the Problem

Sociologists worry about the escalating illegitimate birth rate and the alarming spread of venereal diseases. Scientists and doctors search for cures and for more effective means of birth control. Yet at the root of both these problems is sexual promiscuity. In public discussions of these subjects, seldom is chastity proposed as a solution. Man wants to live without restraints, but avoid the consequences. It simply is not possible.

The American public expresses its outrage at the growing problem of child abuse and sexual molestation. But is such behavior really very surprising in a sex-crazed society that exalts moral perversion on television, in movies and magazines — where pornography is pumped wholesale into the living rooms of America?

The sin of a self-centered lifestyle comes back on both individuals and society. The Scriptures declare that God will send confusion, rebuke, even ruin, upon the nation that forsakes Him. "All the nations will ask, 'Why has the Lord done this to the land?' And the answer will be, 'It is because this people abandoned the covenant of the Lord, the God of their fathers.' " Civilizations do not just die. Their leaders and people are first deceived; then they are destroyed by God.

"Let no man deceive you with vain words: for because of these things [immorality, covetousness, worship of false gods, etc.] cometh the wrath of God upon the children of disobedience" (Eph. 5:6). The deception comes in the form of "the lie": "God shall send them strong delusion, that they should believe the lie" (2 Thess. 2:11). "The lie" was first given to Eve in the garden of Eden: "...ye shall be as gods, knowing [deciding for yourselves] good and evil" (Gen. 3:5).

When a Nation Listens to "The Lie"...

It dethrones God and deifies man's achievements. It exalts human reason as supreme. It trusts education and science to solve its problems. It believes that man is evolving into perfection. It replaces God's moral standards with situational ethics. It promotes sensual pleasure and instant gratification. It strives for a whole utopia of prosperity and peace. It makes the State the sovereign dictator over everyone.

——————————— * ———————————

WHY DID THE ROMAN EMPIRE FALL?

The events which led to the collapse of the Roman Empire are startlingly similar to the events which are occurring in our nation today.

Historical Sequence

1. **Strong Families:** Rome was founded on high moral standards. Each father was respected as the head of the family. In the early republic, the father had legal authority to discipline rebellious members of his family.

2. **Home Education:** The education of the children was the responsibility of the parents. This further strengthened the children's honor and respect for their parents and also deepened the communication and understanding between parents and children.

3. **Prosperity:** Strong Roman families produced a strong nation. The Roman armies were victorious in war. The wealth of conquered nations increased Roman prosperity and prestige.

4. **National Achievements:** Great building programs began in Rome. A vast network of roads united the empire. Magnificent palaces, public buildings and coliseums were constructed.

5. **Infiltration of "the lie":** As Roman families prospered, it became fashionable to hire educated Greeks to care for the children. Greek philosophy, with its humanistic and godless base, was soon passed on to the Roman families. Women demanded more rights and, in order to accommodate them, new marriage contracts were designed, including "open marriages."

6. **Big Government:** By the first century A.D. the father had lost his legal authority. It was delegated to the village, then to the city, then to the state, and finally to the empire. In Rome, citizens complained about housing shortages, soaring rents, congested traffic, polluted air, crime in the streets, and the high cost of

living. Unemployment was a perennial problem. To solve it, the government created a multitude of civil-service jobs, including building inspectors, health inspectors and tax collectors.

7. Decline and Persecution: The problem of big government only multiplied. Meanwhile, a flourishing New Testament Church was established in the Roman Empire through the preaching of the Apostle Paul and others. The final act of the Roman Empire was to bring great persecution to these Christians. Rome was quite tolerant of all religions except Christianity. Christianity was banned and Christians were persecuted, burned, and thrown to the lions. Why? Because the very nature of Christianity is intolerant of "the lie" of Satan which is the basis of every other religion. By the third century, Christianity conquered pagan Rome.

——————————— * ———————————

THE RUINS OF GREECE

A civilization which rejected God and worshipped the human mind and body.

The basic philosophy of Greece was, "Man is the measure of all things. Man, not the gods; the relative, not the absolute."

The Greeks were committed to building the ideal society. Their three commandments were, "Honor the gods, help your friends, and adorn your city." Only the strong survived in Greece. Deformed or weak children were hurled from cliffs or abandoned by their fathers to die. Seven-year-old boys were sent off to learn war. The human body was idolized. A man who could not swim or wrestle was scorned.

As immorality increased, the human mind became supreme. Reason itself was worshipped. The Greeks' search for knowledge was unending. Their probing produced a pantheon of skeptics, cynics, stoics and epicureans. Greek scholars laid the foundations for the study of biology, physiology and anatomy. Their attempt to integrate bodily ills and the psyche was the beginning of psychiatry. Athens also had tax-financed medicare.

Soon the government became a bureaucracy bound in red tape and taxation. At one time there were 218 taxes. There was even a tax on tax receipts. God's judgment came upon the Greek civilization according to the promise of His Word. "The wicked shall be turned into hell, and all the nations that forgot God" (Ps. 9:17).

*Excerpts taken from, *The Rebirth of America*, The Arthur S. DeMoss Foundation, God's Judgment on Nations, pages 141-144.

Foreword

We are living upon the threshold of a historical landmark in the Church Age. For this reason, I have always considered myself extremely fortunate to be able to serve God in these critical times. In these last days, God is moving mightily by His Spirit and is commanding us to arise, to cross over, to engage in battle, and to possess the land. God is raising up a great army to accomplish His purposes in our generation.

Dick Bernal is a hungry young tiger, whom God has raised up to purge the skies and pull down strongholds. He walks on the front lines and on the cutting edge of this awesome move of God to destroy the works of the enemy. His first book, *Storming Hell's Brazen Gates*, was birthed when he and Dr. Dennis Kim (my 'Timothy' and a prominent lawyer whom I sent to help build Pastor Bernal's Jubilee Christian Center in San Jose, California), were flying into Korea for our annual Church Growth International Conference. Dick experienced a great inspiration from the Lord regarding city taking and the pulling down of strongholds. I believe the principles that Dick Bernal has outlined in this new book can revolutionize and empower the church of America to rise up and take the land!

My ministry started with city taking. When I first pioneered my church, nobody would come to our old, torn marine tent because there was great demonic oppression over the village. The key to breaking that bondage was the casting out of a demon from a woman who had lain paralyzed for seven years. When, after months of prayer, the demon oppressing her was cast out and she was healed, our church exploded with growth.

The sky above the village was broken open and the blessings of God began pouring down. Today, the Yoido Full Gospel Church is still growing. We are now in excess of 600,000 members and we are marching forward to our goal of one million members by the year 1992.

The growth of our church and the growth of Christianity throughout the nation of Korea did not come by accident. It came through fervent, violent, prevailing prayer. As Jesus said in Matthew 11:12, "The kingdom of heaven suffers violence, and the violent take it by force." For example, in our church we have all night prayer meetings every single evening where thousands come to pray. On Friday evenings, more than fifteen thousand people join hearts and hands to pray for the Kingdom of God to come. On Prayer Mountain, at least three thousand people are praying, fasting, and ministering unto the Lord on any given day. In all, one-and-a-half million people visit and pray there in any given year. This is not limited only to our church; all over South Korea Christians are praying. One of the most unique characteristics of the Korean church is that millions gather early every morning at 5:30 AM to pray, despite wind, rain or snow.

Great sacrifices were made by the Korean church. The Kingdom of God indeed suffered violence. There was a long history of persecuting Christians by the Communists, as well as by the Japanese occupation forces. For instance, the Japanese installed Shinto altars in all Christian churches. The military police stood guard to enforce the law that required all Christians to bow down to the Shinto altar before entering to worship Almighty God. Those who refused were jailed and punished severely, with many ministers being executed at the hands of the Japanese forces. Many churches corporately decided to oppose this injustice. Many such churches were locked, with women and children inside, and burned to the ground due to their refusal to worship idols. Until recently, it took great sacrifice to be a Christian in Korea. Believers were a minority. But now, because "the blood of the martyrs is the seed of the church," we count at least one-fourth of our nation to be believers in the Lord Jesus Christ.

Finally, a word of admonition. It is so necessary for those who are called to engage in this spiritual warfare to be holy and sanctified, because He is a holy God. Many who have cast out demons, who have prophesied, and who have done wonders in His Name may find God declaring, "Depart from me you who practice lawlessness, I never knew you." The devil has crept into the Church and promoted iniquity, lawlessness and unrighteousness in our midst.

It breaks my heart to see so many co-workers for the Kingdom falling in disgrace. Like the seven sons of Sceva, the evil spirit leapt upon them, overpowered them, prevailed against them, and they fled out of their homes naked and wounded. Without holiness and sanctification, without great sacrifice, and without a fervent prayer life, many will be so wounded. The evil spirit will answer, "Jesus I know, Paul I know, but who are you?"

It would do us well to be admonished by the great Apostle Paul: "Finally, my brethren, be strong in the Lord and in the power of His might. Put on the whole armor of God, that you may be able to stand against the wiles of the devil. For we do not wrestle against flesh and blood, but against principalities, against powers, against the rulers of the darkness of this age, against spiritual hosts of wickedness in the heavenly places. Therefore, take up the whole armor of God, that you may be able to withstand in the evil day, and having done all, to stand. Stand, therefore, having girded your waist with truth, having put on the breastplate of righteousness, and having shod your feet with the preparation of the gospel of peace; above all, taking the shield of faith with which you will be able to quench all the fiery darts of the wicked one. And take the helmet of salvation, and the sword of the Spirit, which is the word of God; praying always with all prayer and supplication in the Spirit, being watchful to this end with all perseverance and supplication for all the saints" (Eph. 6:10-18).

Pastor Paul Yonggi Cho
Yoido Full Gospel Church
Seoul, South Korea, 1989

Table of Contents

CHAPTER 1

Changing the Status Quo

How lonely sits the city that was full of people! How like a widow is she, who was great among the nations! The princess among the provinces has become a slave! (Lam. 1:1)

We have become a nation, a planet, of lonely cities held captive by an unseen evil force. Lamentations is the work of a broken-hearted, young prophet named Jeremiah. This man of God constantly warned the inhabitants of Jerusalem that if they continued to worship other gods, false gods, their city would be destroyed and they would be taken captive. Like most today, they scoffed at the Word of the Lord and that led ultimately to their deportation to Babylon — interestingly enough, the very birth place of the false gods they worshipped! Whoever or whatever has our heart, our affections, our interests, has our worship. We are drawn close to and take on the very nature of that which we worship.

And you He made alive, who were dead in trespasses and sins, in which you once walked according to the course of this world, according to the prince of the power of the air, the spirit who now works in the sons of disobedience, among whom also we all once conducted ourselves in the lusts of our flesh, fulfilling the desires of the flesh and of the mind, and were by NATURE children of wrath, just as the others (Eph. 2:1-3).

But the Bible also tells us:

Grace and peace be multiplied to you in the knowledge of God and of Jesus our Lord, as His divine power has given to us all things that pertain unto life and godliness, through the knowledge of Him who called us by glory and virtue, by which have been given to us exceedingly great and precious promises, that through these you may be partakers of the DIVINE NATURE, having escaped the corruption that is in the world through lust (2 Pet. 1:2-4).

Jeremiah's greatest challenge came from the false prophets who proclaimed that all was well, "Saying, 'Peace, peace!' When there is no peace" (Jer. 8:11). There is nothing more dangerous than a false sense of security that God condones the actions of a nation which worships pleasure, success, sports, entertainment — the list of our idols goes on. We as a people have this insatiable appetite for knowledge, information, scientific break-through, yet we rarely consult the Bible, the Revelation of life's great mysteries, and call it a "piece of antiquated literature" reserved for "the religious crowd."

What has happened to us? Our city streets are rampant with violence, lusts, addictions; they are filled with burned-out, over-stressed people who have no vision. Why has confusion and despair replaced hope and desire?

The plain and simple truth is this: Where there is idolatry you'll find the spirit or principality of confusion, producing confused governments, confused militaries, economies and cit-izens. For example, India is the most confused nation I have ever visited. No wonder, for they worship over 300 million gods! In a crusade there in which I was involved a few years ago, we had absolute chaos each night just trying to get some kind of order in our services. The people couldn't even form simple lines so that we could minister to the sick and afflicted. The airport was such a place of total confusion I'd like to soon forget it. And, checking into a hotel was an adventure all in itself! No one seemed to have the ability to make a decision. The people seemed like cattle moving about aimlessly. Could it be that they were becoming somewhat like the things which they worshipped?

Similarly in many South American countries where the Cath-olics are heavily into idolatry, it is evident that the ruling prince is confusion.

2

The same is true around the world. The six o'clock news is constantly informing us of governmental changes, military coups, and hostile takeovers by some new regime somewhere. People are so confused they think this is normal.

Isaiah predicts just such confusion:

> They shall be ashamed and also disgraced, all of them; they shall go into confusion together, who are makers of idols (Is. 45:16).

Also in the last part of verse 29, chapter 41, he adds emphatically,

> ...their molded images are wind and confusion.

When Paul came to Ephesus, perhaps the most idolatrous city in which he ever ministered with the exception of Athens, he created no small commotion. The prince of confusion over the city of Ephesus knew he had met his match in Paul and tried his best to make the people destroy this great threat to his territory.

> For a certain man named Demetrius, a silversmith, who made silver shrines of Diana, brought no small profit to the craftsmen. He called them together with the workers of similar occupation, and said: "Men, you know that we have our prosperity by this trade. Moreover you see and hear that not only at Ephesus, but throughout almost all Asia, this Paul has persuaded and turned away many people, saying that they are not gods which are made with hands. So not only is this trade of ours in danger of falling into disrepute, but also the temple of the great goddess Diana may be despised and her magnificence destroyed, whom all Asia and the world worship." And when they heard this, they were full of wrath and cried out, saying, "Great is Diana of the Ephesians!" So the whole city was filled with CONFUSION, and rushed into the theater with one accord, having seized Gaius and Aristarchus, Macedonians, Paul's travel companions (Acts 19:24-29).

It is so beautiful to see confusion leave a new convert and peace with soundness of mind take over. "For God is not the author of confusion but of peace, as in all the churches of the saints" (1 Cor. 14:33).

God Himself is the solution to all the world's turmoil, strife and confusion. He is still the Blessed Controller of all things (1 Tim. 6:15). The precious blood still cleanses; the powerful Word still cuts; and the Sovereign Spirit still convicts. But God works through His people, the Church. He needs Spirit-anointed proclaimers and Spirit-filled believers who will confidently claim what is theirs by inheritance in Christ. God has given His people all they need to live godly, victorious lives (2 Pet. 1:3,4). He has given them all they need to wage warfare (Eph. 6:10-17) and tear down strongholds (2 Cor. 10:4-5). We are armed and should be *DANGEROUS!*

Yet, sadly, strangely, many believers are not causing much havoc to the enemy, some are on the sidelines waving flags, and others are just missing in action. This book, following my first book on this general subject, *Storming Hell's Brazen Gates*, calls for courageous action, warfare-waging faith, and all-conquering love. Through biblical case studies of various cities that were "stormed" and taken, it suggests simple strategies for city-taking, for kingdom-building. The church needs to become armed and DANGEROUS!

Lead on, Oh King Eternal... we follow, not with fear!

CHAPTER 2

The High Places

For we wrestle not against flesh and blood, but against principalities, against powers, against the rulers of the darkness of this world, against spiritual wickedness in HIGH PLACES (Eph. 6:12 —KJV).

One of Satan's best kept secrets is the importance of the "high places" in the spirit world. Recently a demon spoke through an individual in Argentina and proudly announced, "I'm from San Francisco and there are millions of us there." The church's ignorance of the ruling spirits in the "high places" over our cities must thrill the powers of darkness.

The word of the Lord came to Moses for the people of Israel, warning them about erecting or leaving high places dedicated to idols.

I will destroy your high places, cut down your incense altars, and cast your carcasses on the lifeless forms of your idols; and my soul shall abhor you. I will lay your cities waste and bring your sanctuaries to desolation, and I will not smell the fragrance of your sweet aromas. I will bring the land to desolation, and your enemies who dwell in it shall be astonished at it. I will scatter you among the nations and draw out a sword after you; your land shall be desolate and your cities waste (Lev. 26:30-33).

Satan knows that man for the most part is incurably religious; he will worship something. Is it little wonder that the first two commandments are "You shall have no other gods before me," and, "You shall not make for yourself any carved image, or any

5

likeness of anything that is in heaven above, or that is in the earth beneath, or that is in the water under the earth; you shall not bow down to them nor serve them. For I, the Lord your God, am a jealous God, visiting the iniquity of the fathers on the children to the third and fourth generations of those who hate Me..." (Ex. 20:3-5).

A. W. Pink in his book, *Gleanings from Exodus*, page 161, says,

> *If this first commandment received the respect it demands, obedience to the other nine would follow as a matter of course. Thou shalt have no other object of worship: Thou shalt own no other authority as absolute: Thou shalt make me supreme in your hearts and lives. How much this first commandment contains! There are other "gods" besides idols of wood and stone. Money, pleasure, fashion, fame, gluttony and a score of other things which usurp the rightful place of God in the affections and thoughts of many. It is not without reason that even to the saints the exhortation is given.*

God's people are to give "no place," no "high place," to the devil! The Apostle John warns,

> *Little children, keep yourselves from idols* (1 Jn. 5:21).

Israel became a great nation under the leadership of King David and his son and heir, King Solomon. God greatly blessed and prospered His people Israel as they followed after Him, but Solomon gave place to the devil. It probably started off innocently like most sin does, but, left unchecked, it led to destruction. Solomon loved many foreign women, and that was not only his downfall but the beginning of the end for Israel as a nation, causing them to transgress the laws of God and as a consequence fall into bondage.

The Lord warned Solomon clearly about this pernicious process in 1 Kings 9:6-9:

> *But if you or your sons at all turn from following Me, and do not keep My commandments and My statutes which I have set before you, but go and serve other gods and worship*

them, then I will cut off Israel from the land which I have given them; and this house which I have sanctified for My name I will cast out of My sight. Israel will be a proverb and a byword among all peoples. And this house will be exalted; yet everyone who passes by it will be astonished and will hiss, and say, "Why has the Lord done thus to this land and to this house?" Then will they answer, "Because they forsook the Lord their God, who brought their fathers out of the land of Egypt, and have embraced other gods, and worshipped them and served them; therefore the Lord has brought all this calamity on them."

Commenting on Solomon's downfall, *The Pulpit Commentary* states: "We have already heard of the multiplication of silver and gold (ch. 10:14-25), in defiance of Deuteronomy 17:17, and of the multiplication of horses (ch. 10:27-29), in disregard of verse 16 of the same chapter. We now read (ch. 11:1-8) how the ruin of this great prince was completed by the multiplication of wives" (*The Pulpit Commentary*, MacDonald Publishing Company, First Kings, p. 220).

Apparently Solomon had become addicted to the sexual favors his foreign wives were giving him and, as often happens, became blinded through a spirit of lust. "Many a man has had his heart pierced and his head broken by his own rib" (ibid, p. 226). Solomon not only allowed his wives to continue in idolatrous worship, but he also built "high places" for their demon gods, where he himself "... went after Ashtoreth, Milcom and Chemosh" (1 Kings 11:5-8).

One of the more fascinating Scriptures concerning Solomon which demands close scrutiny is 1 Kings 11:4, which says,

For it was so, when Solomon was old, that his wives turned his heart after other gods; and his heart was not loyal to the Lord his God, as was the heart of his father David.

While the ancient adage, "It's hard to teach an old dog new tricks" generally rings true, in Solomon's case the old dog did learn new tricks. The compromising choices of youth betrayed

7

him in old age, compounding his disobedience and contributing to his final fall. How important it is to make right choices in youth, and how important to teach our children to resist the devil while they are strong in spirit, soul and body!

Sadly, when Solomon fell, he did not fall alone. When a king falls, how many fall with him! Often, as in Solomon's case, he takes a whole nation with him.

The slow but steady downfall of Israel, which became a divided kingdom upon Solomon's death, is well documented in 1 and 2 Kings, as well as 1 and 2 Chronicles. For the most part the monarchs who followed him were wicked and did evil in God's sight. But even with the exceptional few who did "right in the sight of the Lord," there was one particularly grievous oversight.

Let's trace it, starting with Asa, the son of Abijam, in 1 Kings 15:11-13:

> *Asa did what was right in the eyes of the Lord, as did his father David. And he banished the perverted persons from the land and removed all the idols that his father made. Also he removed Maachah his grandmother from being queen mother, because she made an obscene image of Asherah. And Asa cut down her obscene image and burned it by the Brook Kidron.*

Notice that while Asa was a good king, he did not remove all the unauthorized places of worship:

> *But the high places were not removed. Nevertheless Asa's heart was loyal to the Lord all his days* (1 Kings 15:14).

Next look at King Jehoash in 2 Kings 12:1-3:

> *In the seventh year of Jehu, Jehoash became king, and he reigned forty years in Jerusalem. His mother's name was Zibiah of Beersheba. Jehoash did what was right in the sight of the Lord all the days in which Jehoiada the priest instructed him. But the high places were not taken away; the people still sacrificed and burned incense on the high places.*

Again, a good man, but the "high places" were not removed. The same goes for king Amaziah (2 Kings 14:1-4) and king

8

Azariah (2 Kings 15:1-4); even king Jehosaphat didn't take away the "high places" (2 Chron. 20:31-33).

A similar situation exists in America today. Our nation has literally thousands of churches pastored by good, God-fearing men who want desperately to follow their Lord and do what is right in His sight, but they are not removing, pulling down, the "high places" over their cities. And I'm not talking about man-made "high rises" but about princes, dark powers, and rulers in the heavenlies against whom we wrestle in spiritual conflict.

In Ephesians 2:2 Paul refers to Satan as the "prince of the power of the air." As I point out in my book, *Storming Hell's Brazen Gates*, Prince or ARCHON in the Greek means: to be number one, a ruler or magistrate. Satan is number one in all that kills, steals or destroys. He is the number-one liar, deceiver, inflicter of fear and doubt.

He is also the "power of the air" (Eph. 2:2). The word *power* expresses the idea of force, capacity, control, jurisdiction and strength. *Air* means exactly what it says, "air," that which we breathe, the atmosphere which engulfs the earth. I have noticed in my travels around the globe that where there is much demon activity in a city or nation, or perhaps a spirit of oppression as in Communist countries, it is harder to breathe.

I was sharing this observation with a friend of mine, a former Billy Graham crusade director, and he recalled that several years ago when he was visiting a certain country in South America which at that time was under a heavy military government, the air always seemed stuffy and thick. He simply wrote it off as humidity mixed with smog. Recently, however, he returned to the same country, which had switched to a more democratic form of government and in which the church was experiencing a major spiritual awakening. My friend reported, "When I got off the airplane, I could immediately tell that something in the spirit realm had changed just by breathing the air. It felt light and breezy."

CHAPTER 3

Cities for the Taking

Shout! for the Lord has given you the city! (Josh. 6:16)

God loves cities. He loves your city. There is no city too tough for God to crack. The Bible is full of examples of seemingly impossible cities where the glory of God broke through.

What is a city anyway?

Simply defined, a city is an organized population concentrated in one place. I'm told that nearly 80% of the earth's population live in or very close to a city. A city is a place where people basically live off people, which creates a challenge for the body of Christ in getting folks to depend on God as their Source, not man. I heard a preacher say that the Bible was really the story of two cities in conflict: the city of Zion versus the city of Babylon; or, one could say, the people of God against the spirit of Antichrist. Jesus refers to believers as a city:

> *You are the light of the world. A city that is set on a hill cannot be hidden* (Mt. 5:14).

Why do you suppose that some of the most beautiful cities on earth are some of the most wicked, i.e., Rio de Janero, Miami, Hong Kong, San Francisco, Paris, Rome, London, Buenos Aires, to name just a few? Satan is used to beauty. He loves pretty things and he wants so desperately to be like God who surrounds Himself with splendor and grace.

As beautiful as earth's cities are, none compare to the one God is presently building for His people.

The city of God

Then one of the seven angels who had the seven bowls filled with the seven last plagues came to me and talked with me, saying, "Come, I will show you the bride, the Lamb's wife." And he carried me away in the Spirit to a great and high mountain, and showed me the great city, the holy Jerusalem, descending out of heaven from God, having the glory of God. And her light was like a most precious stone, like a jasper stone, clear as crystal. Also she had a great and high wall with twelve gates, and twelve angels at the gates, the names written on them, which are the names of the twelve tribes of the children of Israel: three gates on the east, three gates on the north, three gates on the south, and three gates on the west. Now the wall of the city had twelve foundations, and on them were the names of the twelve apostles of the Lamb. And he who talked with me had a gold reed to measure the city, its gates, and its walls. And the city is laid out as a square and its length is as great as its breadth. And he measured the city with the reed: twelve thousand furlongs. Its length, breadth, and height are equal. Then he measured its wall: one hundred and forty-four cubits, according to the measure of a man, that is, of an angel. And the construction of its wall was of jasper; and the city was pure gold like clear glass. And the foundations of the wall of the city were adorned with all kinds of precious stones: the first foundation was jasper, the second sapphire, the third chalcedony, the fourth emerald, the fifth sardonyx, the sixth sardius, the seventh chrysolite, the eighth beryl, the ninth topaz, the tenth chrysoprase, the eleventh jacinth, and the twelfth amethyst. And the twelve gates were twelve pearls: each individual gate was of one pearl. And the street of the city was pure gold, like transparent glass.

But I saw no temple in it, for the Lord God Almighty and the Lamb are its temple. And the city had no need of the sun or of the moon to shine in it, for the glory of God illuminated it, and the Lamb is its light. And the nations of those who are saved shall walk in its light, and the kings of the earth bring

*their glory and honor into it. Its gates shall not be shut at all
by day (there shall be no night there). And they shall bring the
glory and the honor of the nations into it. But there shall by
no means enter it anything that defiles, or causes an abomination or a lie, but only those who are written in the Lamb's
Book of Life* (Rev. 21:9-27).

NOW THAT'S A CITY!

The History of Cities

The first man to build a city was, strangely enough, Cain, a
fugitive and a vagabond who murdered his younger brother
Abel over an offering. In a jealous rage, full of rejection and hate,
he took his brother's life. God placed a curse upon Cain, which is
described in Genesis 4:11-17:

*So now you are cursed from the earth, which has opened
its mouth to receive your brother's blood from your hand.
When you till the ground, it shall no longer yield its strength to
you. A fugitive and a vagabond you shall be on the earth. And
Cain said to the Lord, "My punishment is greater than I can
bear! Surely you have driven me out this day from the face of
the ground; I shall be hidden from Your face; I shall be a
fugitive and a vagabond on the earth, and it will happen that
anyone who finds me will kill me." And the Lord said to him,
"Therefore, whoever kills Cain, vengeance shall be taken on
him sevenfold." And the Lord set a mark on Cain, lest anyone
finding him should kill him.*

*Then Cain went out from the presence of the Lord and
dwelt in the land of Nod on the east of Eden. And Cain knew
his wife, and she conceived and bore Enoch. And he built a
city, and called the name of the city after the name of his son
— Enoch.*

He built a city! Imagine, the father of the modern city was a
paranoid killer who constructed a city (more like a fort) to defy
God's curse that he would be a wanderer and nomad! Nomads
don't build cities; agriculturists do. The scriptural record makes
it clear that Cain feared for his life (Gen. 4:14). It states further,
"Cain went out from the presence of the Lord" (vs. 16).

13

Let me ask you a question. When was the last time you were downtown? Not out in the suburbs where the malls and schools are, but deep in the heart of your city? What did you feel in your spirit when you were walking the streets of the inner city? The absence of God's presence, I would venture to say. Our inner cities are choked with prostitutes, drug dealers and weird bookstores selling perversion or black arts; with people talking to themselves and stumbling down the sidewalk; with derelicts and reprobates hitting up every passer-by for a buck to buy cheap wine. And no one ever looks you in the eye! That's the spirit of Cain which stalks the inner city. Ever notice how few successful churches are found in these places? It's a satanic stronghold, and Satan's power must be broken before light will fill the city. If it isn't, the gangs of the inner city will soon spill out into the suburbs. But fear not, for the Lord is a city-taking God!

In striking contrast to Cain and his spirit of fear, we come next to Nimrod in Genesis 10:8-12. Nimrod was anything but fearful. "He was a mighty hunter *against* the Lord," is a better translation of verse 9. This great-grandson of Noah was brash, arrogant, and godless. In verse 10 you will notice the word "kingdom" used for the first time in Scripture. "And the beginning of his kingdom was Babel (Babylon)..." Apparently his kingdom was made up of cities. Some like Nineveh were very large and important cities.

Genesis 11:4 describes the epitome of man's self-adulation. "And they said, 'Come let us build ourselves a city, and a tower whose top is in the heavens; let us make a name for ourselves, lest we be scattered abroad over the face of the whole earth.' "

The next time you are in a major city take a good look at the skyscrapers. Notice the names on them — men's names glorifying their personal kingdoms, family names, corporate names. These modern towers of Babel reaching toward the heavens flaunt their independence from God Almighty. Not only are we dealing with the spirit of Cain in our cities, but also the spirit of Nimrod. The fearful and anxious rub elbows with the proud and boastful.

Sodom and Gomorrah

Next we come to the twin cities of Sodom and Gomorrah. The awful stench of their perversion offended the nostrils of a Holy God and demanded punishment, but Abraham stood in the gap for the sinners. He illustrates one of the fundamental principles in city taking: Intercession. The biblical account is poignant.

And Abraham came near and said, "Would you also destroy the righteous with the wicked? Suppose there were fifty righteous within the city; would You also destroy the place and not spare it for the fifty righteous that were in it? Far be it from You to do such a thing as this, to slay the righteous with the wicked, so that the righteous should be as the wicked; far be it from You! Shall not the Judge of all the earth do right?" And the Lord said, "If I find in Sodom fifty righteous within the city, then I will spare all the place for their sakes." Then Abraham answered and said, "Indeed now, I who am but dust and ashes have taken it upon myself to speak to the Lord: Suppose there were five less than the fifty righteous; would You destroy all of the city for lack of five?" And He said, "If I find there forty-five, I will not destroy it." Then he spoke to Him yet again and said, "Suppose there should be forty found there?" And He said, "I will not do it for the sake of forty." And he said, "Let not the Lord be angry, and I will speak; suppose thirty should be found there?" And He said, "I will not do it if I find thirty there." Then he said, "Indeed now, I have taken it upon myself to speak to the Lord: Suppose twenty should be found there?" And He said, "I will not destroy it for the sake of twenty." And he said, "Let not the Lord be angry and I will speak but once more: Suppose ten should be found there?" And He said, "I will not destroy it for the sake of ten." So the Lord went went His way as soon as He had finished speaking with Abraham; and Abraham returned to his place (Gen. 18:23-33).

Abraham interceded not simply for the rescue of Lot from the doomed cities but also for the salvation of the cities themselves, with their miserable inhabitants.

Oh, Christian friend, how we have lost the wonder of compassion! Abraham did not blindly shut his eyes to the Sodomites, as many do today, on the plea that they deserved whatever fate God had for them. Nor did Abraham shrug his shoulders and say, "Hey, what can one man do for a place so vile?" Instead, he drew himself near to God with an almost venturesome audacity in prayer.

To emphasize the logic of his argument, I quote again from *The Pulpit Commentary*, Book of Genesis, Part III, Homiletics, p. 251:

> *The principle on which the patriarch stands is not the grace of the covenant, but the righteousness of the Judge. His meaning is that in moral goodness there is a certain dynamic force which operates towards the preservation of the wicked, and which the Divine righteousness itself is bound to take into its calculations.*

Think of it! God was willing to spare two wicked cities like Sodom and Gomorrah because His covenant man stood as a mediator and pleaded with Him. Ten, just ten righteous, would have done the trick. Living where I do in Silicon Valley and pastoring in the shadow of San Francisco, there are times I wonder what is holding back another quake like that of 1906. It's a city full of blatantly open Sodomites, and even a large percentage of the clergy have professed to being homosexual or at least bisexual. What's keeping back the arm of judgment? The compassionate intercessors who love San Francisco! The haunting question persists, where are the Abrahams of today? We need them now more than ever!

How not to take a city

I don't want to dwell on the negative side of things, yet I feel compelled to share at least one case in which cities weren't taken by the generation under Moses' leadership. Let's pick up the story in Numbers 13:17-33.

> *So Moses sent them to spy out the land of Canaan, and said to them, "Go up this way into the South, and go up to the mountains, and see what the land is like: whether the people*

who dwell in it are strong or weak, few or many; whether the land they dwell in is good or bad; whether the cities they inhabit are like camps or strongholds; whether the land is rich or poor; and whether there are forests there or not. Be of good courage. And bring some of the fruit of the land." Now the time was the season of the first ripe grapes. So they went up and spied out the land from the Wilderness of Zin as far as Rehob, near the entrance of Hamath. And they went up through the South and came to Hebron; Ahiman, Sheshai, and Talmai, the descendants of Anak, were there. (Now Hebron was built seven years before Zoan in Egypt). Then they came to the Valley of Eshcol, and there cut down a branch with one cluster of grapes; they carried it between two of them on a pole. They also brought some of the pomegranates and figs. The place was called the Valley of Eshcol, because of the cluster which the men of Israel cut down there. And they returned from spying out the land after forty days. So they departed and came back to Moses and Aaron and all the congregation of the children of Israel in the Wilderness of Paran, at Kadesh; they brought back word to them and to all the congregation, and showed them the fruit of the land. Then they told him, and said: "We went to the land where you sent us. It truly flows with milk and honey, and this is its fruit. Nevertheless the people who dwell in the land are strong; the cities are fortified and very large; moreover we saw the descendants of Anak there. The Amalekites dwell in the land of the South; the Hittites, the Jebusites, and the Amorites dwell in the mountains; and the Canaanites dwell by the sea and along the banks of the Jordan." Then Caleb quieted the people before Moses and said, "Let us go up at once and take possession, for we are well able to overcome it." But the men who had gone up with him said, "We are not able to go up against the people, for they are stronger than we." And they gave the children of Israel a bad report of the land which they had spied out, saying, "The land through which we have gone as spies is a land that devours its inhabitants, and all the people whom we saw in it are men of great stature. There we saw the giants (the descendants of Anak came from the

17

*giants); and we were like grasshoppers in our own sight, and
so we were in their sight."*

Okay, where did Moses miss it? First of all, God had already
told him (and the people) all about the land:

*For the Lord your God is bringing you into a good land, a land
of brooks of water, of fountains and springs, that flow out of
valleys and hills; a land of wheat and barley, of vines and fig trees
and pomegranates, a land of olive oil and honey; a land in which
you will eat bread without scarcity, in which you will lack nothing;
a land whose stones are iron and out of whose hills you can dig
copper* (Deut. 8:7-9).

Secondly, God didn't ask Moses to find out if the inhabitants
were strong or weak, few or many, or what condition the cities
and camps were in. But undoubtedly his biggest mistake was
allowing the ten spineless spies to cast their vote of fear and
doubt. By doing so, the heart of God's people melted and they
wept and cried out against Moses, Aaron, Joshua and Caleb. As
a result, not only did they waste 40 years, but also all the men
over twenty years of age lost their lives (Num. 14:29).

When God speaks clearly, we follow His instructions implic-
itly. We don't add to nor take away from our marching orders.
Nor do we vote on it. More cities in America have gone to the
devil while church elders sit in the back room voting on everything from carpet colors to softball uniforms for the youth group.

Those that have a different spirit like Caleb, a strong spirit, a
city-taking spirit will inherit the land! (Num. 14:24)

CHAPTER 4

Jericho: Key to Conquest

The forty years the children of Israel spent wandering in the wilderness was not a total loss. God was making soldiers out of slaves, a task He is still undertaking today with all of His delivered ones. It didn't take long to get His people out of Egypt, but it took years to get Egypt out of His people!

Finally, the Lord was ready to send them into the promised land, a land of blessing and provision, but also a land with many challenges, the first being a mighty walled city, the city of Jericho.

The First Encounter

Some have concluded that Joshua erred in sending the two spies into Jericho to get a layout of the land. The critics maintain that Joshua should have trusted wholly in the Lord and not followed the example of Moses which led to an evil report from the ten spies, with only Joshua and Caleb standing in faith. Let me remind you, however, that it was God's idea to spy out the land, not Moses!

And the Lord spoke to Moses, saying, "Send men to spy out the land of Canaan, which I am giving to the children of Israel; from each tribe of their fathers you shall send a man, every one a leader among them" (Num. 13:1-2).

We should also remember that Joshua was one of the spies and apparently saw merit in, "looking before one leaps"!

Now Joshua the son of Nun sent out two men from Acacia Grove to spy secretly, saying, "Go, view the land, especially

Jericho." So they went, and came to the house of the harlot named Rahab, and lodged there (Josh. 2:1).

We saw that in Sodom and Gomorrah's case, intercession and "drawing near to God in the spirit" worked wonders and nearly saved two rotten-to-the-core cities. Lot and his family were rescued. Although Lot's wife's deliverance was short-lived, God still honored Abraham's request.

But prayer alone is not enough. It is the beginning of city-taking. It is preparing and planning in the Spirit, getting the mind and strategy of Christ on just how to penetrate a city with the gospel.

Spying out the land is essential when warring for a city. Most Christians know how to get from their home to church, to the store, to the malls, or to a friend's house. But how many really know their city? Christians should walk or drive every major freeway, avenue and road of their cities, praying and coming against demonic strongholds over every neighborhood.

I have had the privilege of being raised in San Jose and have watched this sleepy little agricultural town explode into the heart of Silicon Valley. I have this city in my heart. I know it! I know its people! I have my hand on the pulse of it, monitoring each beat. I am constantly keeping surveillance over changes which affect its flow. Make no mistake, knowing your city is a necessary first step in taking your city for Christ.

A. W. Pink in *Gleanings from Joshua*, p. 52, introduces another intriguing insight in the process of city-taking for God:

The land which Joshua was called upon to conquer was occupied by a fierce, powerful and ungodly people. Humanly speaking, there was no reason to conclude that the Canaanites would render assistance or do ought to make his task easier: rather to the contrary, as the attitude and actions of the kings had shown (Num. 21:1, 23, 33)... When he sent forth the two spies to obtain information about Jericho, he could not naturally expect that any of its inhabitants would render them any help in their difficult task. Yet, that is exactly what happened, for those spies received remarkable favour in the eyes of her (Rahab the harlot) in whose house they obtained lodgment. Not only was she kindly disposed toward them, but she even hazarded her own life on their behalf.

Israel's experience was reminiscent of Proverbs 16:7 which says, "When a man's ways please the Lord, He makes even his enemies to be at peace with him." How gracious is the God we serve!

Believe me, when you move in faith to take your city for the Lord, two things will be true. First, the resistance you will experience is like nothing you've ever come up against before. When you tell the prince over your city, "We're here to take it for God," he will not just play dead; he will violently oppose you! That is why the Lord told Joshua over and over again, "Be strong and of good courage; do not be afraid, nor be dismayed, for the Lord your God is with you wherever you go" (Josh. 1:9).

But, second, it's amazing who will come to your aid to help you win your city. Imagine a prostitute as a key player in conquering Jericho! And what about David's feisty four hundred, "those in distress, everyone who was in debt, and everyone who was discontented... So he became captain over them" (1 Sam. 22:2). And you think your congregation is hurting! Out of David's "maladjusted malcontents" came mighty men who knew how to possess the land promised to them.

Once the city had been surveyed and the scouting party had safely returned, the task of crossing the Jordan and actually taking the city had to be undertaken. Remember, Moses and the old school had died off. A new, younger generation stood at the Jordan. I'm finding out that it is this new, fearless generation today that is willing to take on a whole city. The older, established churches are far too busy retaining the status quo and do not like their comfortable boat rocked with all this talk of spiritual conquest and warfare.

Then Joshua rose early in the morning; and they set out from Acacia Grove and came to the Jordan, he and all the children of Israel, and lodged there before they crossed over. So it was, after three days, that the officers went through the

21

camp; and they commanded the people, saying, "When you see the ark of the covenant of the Lord your God, and the priests, the Levites, bearing it, then you shall set out from your place and go after it. Yet there shall be a space between you and it, about two thousand cubits by measure. Do not come near it, that you may know the way by which you must go, for you have not passed this way before." And Joshua said to the people, "Sanctify yourselves for tomorrow the Lord will do wonders among you" (Josh. 3:1-5).

The ark here prefigured Christ as the believer's covenant Guide. The contents of the ark represented the Word, the authority and the provision of the Lord, capped off by a mercy seat. "Let it (the ark) go before you" was the command and "you go after it."

To get ahead of God when trying to win a city could be fatal to a church or a group of churches or a pastor, and even to the sheep. I've noticed in some areas of the world where revival has broken out that there is a high toll of casualties — divorce, sickness, church splits, even death. A price too high to pay for being impetuous.

Before the Lord had Joshua move on Jericho, the nation participated in acts of committal: The erecting of memorial stones (Josh. 4), and the circumcision of all males who hadn't been circumcised in the wilderness (Josh. 5).

Memorial Stones:

And it came to pass, when all the people had completely crossed over the Jordan, that the Lord spoke to Joshua saying: "Take for yourselves twelve men from the people, one man from every tribe, and command them, saying, 'Take for yourselves twelve stones from here, out of the midst of the Jordan, from the place where the priests' feet stood firm. You shall carry them over with you and leave them in the lodging place where you lodge tonight.' " Then Joshua called the twelve men whom he had appointed from the children of Israel, one man from every tribe; and Joshua said to them: "Cross over before the ark of the Lord your God into the

22

midst of the Jordan, and each one of you take up a stone on his shoulder, according to the number of the tribes of the children of Israel, that this may be a sign among you when your children ask in time to come, saying, 'What do these stones mean to you?' Then you shall answer them that the waters of the Jordan were cut off before the ark of the covenant of the Lord; when it crossed over the Jordan, the waters of the Jordan were cut off. And these stones shall be for a memorial to the children of Israel forever" (Josh. 4:1-7).

Circumcision:

So it was, when all the kings of the Amorites who were on the west side of the Jordan, and all the kings of the Canaanites who were by the sea, heard that the Lord had dried up the waters of the Jordan from before the children of Israel until we had crossed over, that their heart melted; and there was no spirit in them any longer because of the children of Israel. At that time the Lord said to Joshua, "Make flint knives for yourself, and circumcise the sons of Israel again the second time." So Joshua made flint knives for himself, and circumcised the sons of Israel at the hill of the foreskins. And this is the reason why Joshua circumcised them: All the people who came out of Egypt who were males, all the men of war, had died in the wilderness on the way, after they had come out of Egypt. For all the people who came out had been circumcised, but all the people who were born in the wilderness on the way as they came out of Egypt had not been circumcised (Josh. 5:1-5).

In ancient times, altars of stone were erected as reminders of some wonderful intervention by God, as memorials to remind coming generations of God's goodness and power toward His people.

The Lord is about to deliver a whole city into the hands of His people Israel, but knowing how prone human hearts are to forget His past interventions, He demanded an altar of remembrance. A passage of Scripture recurring too often in the Old Testament is, "They soon forgot His works" (Ps. 106:13).

23

The Lord held back the waters of the Jordan as a sign and wonder to the heathen and as a reminder to His people that the same God who parted the Red Sea some forty years earlier for Moses was indeed with Joshua in battle. The twelve stones were taken from the bottom of Jordan. Smooth stones, shaped and constantly cleansed by a moving river. These twelve stones represented each tribe, showing God's love and interest not simply in the masses but in individuals. These city-takers had a God who knew them, loved them, would fight for them; a God who took the rough edges off them by a rushing flow of His Spirit.

Before God could turn them loose on Jericho, some important unfinished business needed to be attended to — circumcision! The "circumcising of the sons of Israel again the second time," needs a word of explanation. Obviously, the Scriptures are not suggesting these men needed to be circumcised again, any more than you and I need to be "born again" again! Knowing the importance of circumcision as the token or sign of the covenant with God (Gen. 17:9-11), it is inconceivable that this was a slight oversight on behalf of the children of Israel. Another question arises: How come Moses didn't put his foot down and demand that all males who were born in the wilderness be circumcised. Scholars and commentators have argued over this point for years. Some say, "Sinful neglect." Others suggest, "Because of their frequent journeying and the inconvenience of performing circumcision, they kept putting it off."

Matthew Henry concedes the explanation is found in Numbers 14. "Because of their infidelity and evil hearts, they tasted the breach of His promise; their apostasy and breaking of the covenant releasing Him from His engagement to bring them into Canaan." Circumcision is a type of the mortification of sin and the putting off of the filth of the flesh.

City-takers are going to stir up the enemy's nest. Only the cleansed and sanctified will be victorious in battle. I'm not talking about the hyper-holy, super-do-gooders, but about those who know their God and who do great exploits (Dan. 11:32).

24

The city itself

A key city! A powerful fortress of seemingly impregnable walls! An invisible sign seems to say, "God's people, listen up. You shall go no further. Stop!" If Jericho could be taken, what encouragement it would bring to the children of Israel and what a message it would send to the other cities of Canaan! Think of it! It would be like taking New York, Miami, or Los Angeles, even San Francisco. What a blow to Satan's kingdom! But what joy it would bring to the camp of the redeemed!

Our attitude toward winning a city has been basically to gather at the church for a prayer meeting and bind the devil until we're blue in the face. I believe there is an active side to warfare as well as a passive one. As an old sage once said, "It's time to vitalize the legal." In other words, put feet to our covenant rights and promises.

Only after the Hebrew nation had built a memorial altar, had been circumcised and had kept the Passover, was it time for them to move on the city.

Now Jericho was securely shut up because of the children of Israel; none went out, and none came in. And the Lord said to Joshua: "See! I have given Jericho into your hand, its king and the mighty men of valor. You shall march around the city, all you men of war; you shall go all around the city once. This you shall do six days. And seven priests shall bear seven trumpets of rams' horns before the ark. But the seventh day you shall march around the city seven times, and the priests shall blow the trumpets. Then it shall come to pass, when they make a long blast with the ram's horn, and when you hear the sound of the trumpet, that all the people shall shout with a great shout; then the wall of the city will fall down flat. And the people shall go up every man straight before him." So Joshua the son of Nun called the priests and said to them, "Take up the ark of the covenant, and let seven priests bear seven trumpets of rams' horns before the ark of the Lord." And he said to the people, "Proceed, and march around the city, and let him who is armed advance before the ark of the Lord."

So it was, when Joshua had spoken to the people, that the seven priests bearing the seven trumpets of rams' horns before the Lord advanced and blew the trumpets, the ark of the covenant of the Lord followed them. The armed men went before the priests who blew the trumpets, and the rear guard came after the ark, while the priests continued blowing the trumpets. Now Joshua had commanded the people, saying, "You shall not shout or make any noise with your voice, nor shall any word proceed out of your mouth, until the day I say to you, 'Shout!' Then you shall shout." So he had the ark of the Lord circle the city, going around it once. Then they came into the camp and lodged in the camp.

And Joshua rose early in the morning, and the priests took up the ark of the Lord. Then seven priests bearing seven trumpets of rams' horns before the ark of the Lord went on continually and blew with the trumpets. And the armed men went before them. But the rear guard came after the ark of the Lord, while the priests continued blowing the trumpets. And the second day they marched around the city once and returned to the camp. So they did six days. But it came to pass on the seventh day that they rose early, about the dawning of the day, and marched around the city seven times in the same manner. On that day only they marched around the city seven times. And the seventh time it was so, when the priests blew the trumpets, that Joshua said to the people: "SHOUT, FOR THE LORD HAS GIVEN YOU THE CITY!" (Josh. 6:1-16)

This was far more than human conflict. Jehovah God Himself was waging war against Satan and his hosts! The Canaanites were devoted to idolatry, divination, necromancy, witchcraft, charms and familiar spirits. The children of Israel would be the instruments of God's judgment upon these wicked, perverted people.

When you come into the land which the Lord your God is giving you, you shall not learn to follow the abominations of those nations. There shall not be found among you anyone

*who makes his son or his daughter pass through the fire, or
one who practices witchcraft, or a soothsayer, or one who
interprets omens, or a sorcerer, or one who conjures spells, or
a medium, or a spiritist, or one who calls up the dead. For all
who do these things are an abomination to the Lord, and
because of these abominations the Lord your God drives
them out from before you. You shall be blameless before the
Lord your God. For these nations which you will dispossess
listened to soothsayers and diviners; but as for you, the Lord
your God has not appointed such for you* (Deut. 18:9-14).

These satanic strongholds had to be pulled down, and according to Paul we must do the same.

*But I say that the things which the Gentiles sacrifice they
sacrifice to demons and not to God, and I do not want you to
have fellowship with demons. You cannot drink the cup of
the Lord and the cup of demons; you cannot partake of the
Lord's table and of the table of demons* (1 Cor. 10:20-21).

A key verse to focus on in this whole process of spiritual
warfare is verse 2 of Joshua 6:

*And the Lord said to Joshua: "See, I have given Jericho
into your hands, its king, and the mighty men of valor."*

Immediately we see who gets the credit for the victory. "God
resists the proud, but gives grace to the humble" (Jas. 4:6).

One of the great dangers of spiritual warfare is that it attracts
a lot of attention, especially with people who want to be where
the action is without paying the price. But it is an arena reserved
for skilled veterans who know where their strength comes from.
Those who are the greatest threat to Satan's kingdom are usually
quiet, unassuming types who don't need to be praised or noticed
by the approving crowd. They simply go about their Father's
business, purging the heavenlies of principalities and powers
over their cities.

The game plan

A. W. Pink brings up a good point: "If the Lord had definitely
given Jericho into the hands of Joshua, why were such elaborate

preparations as these necessary for its overthrow?" (*Gleanings from Joshua*, p. 149)

Pink answers his own question.

Let those who feel the force of any such difficulty weigh attentively what we are about to say. In reality, those verses exemplify and illustrate a principle which it is most important for us to apprehend. That principle may be stated thus: the disclosure of God's gracious purpose and the absolute certainty of its accomplishment in no wise renders needless the discharge of our responsibilities. God's assuring us of the sureness of the end does not set aside the indispensability of the use of means. Thus, here again, as everywhere, we see preserved the balance of Truth.

God's promises should never promote inactivity on our part. Many pastors who have read my book, *Storming Hell's Brazen Gates*, have told me, "God has given us our city," yet few have ever shared God's instructions and strategy for conquest with me. One man of God and a dear friend, Ed Silvoso, is an exception.

Ed, the brother-in-law of Luis Palau and Juan Carlos Ortiz, is, like these great preachers, an Argentine. Ed is a thinker, a strategist. He and his team from Harvest Evangelism, a ministry over which he presides, has targeted a city in Northern Argentina. Their street-by-street, block-by-block attack on the ruling princes, followed up with crusades, Bible studies, concerts and personal evangelism is very exciting to me. I wish I were right in the middle of it! Their main focus, once the rest has taken place, is church planting. As Dr. Lester Sumrall expressed it, "Plant a tree where generations after you eat from it."

How strange God's instructions must have sounded to Joshua. Can you imagine the look on the faces of the men in his army when he shared the battle plan! There have been more than a few eyebrows raised over some of my teaching on dethroning the prince over San Jose, California. No one has ever accused God of being orthodox!

Once again, please note the importance of the ark. God's presence was with them as they marched. This was not going to be a victory brought about by the arm of the flesh but by "His Spirit."

And then, the blowing of the trumpets. The Bible has much to say about the significance of the trumpet's blast. We are told to lift up our voices like a trumpet, to sound the alarm, to hearken to its sound, just to name a few.

At Jericho, I'm sure it was used to frighten the enemy as well as to encourage the Israelites. I know beyond a shadow of a doubt that when our church gathers for praise and worship and our band "gets it going" with the brass section wailing away and the saints entering into the high praises of God, the demons shudder and become confused while the children of God are refreshed and strengthened.

The seventh verse of Joshua 6 is very powerful. It isn't just the priests doing the marching or warfare, but also the rank and file. Today we have too many worn-out preachers trying to go it alone. No one shows up at the prayer meetings or joins in a called fast; so the preacher tries it solo. No, that's not God's way. The pattern we see at Jericho is of the priests blowing the trumpet and the people marching. What harmony!

Notice another interesting aspect of their strategy in Joshua 6:10,11.

> Now Joshua had commanded the people, saying, "You shall not shout or make any noise with your voice, nor shall any word proceed out of your mouth, until the day I say to you, 'Shout!' Then you shall shout." So he had the ark of the Lord circle the city, going around it once. Then they came into the camp and lodged in the camp.

Absolute silence! Could it be action really does speak louder than words? Someone asked Kenneth E. Hagin once why he didn't talk much. He replied, "The less to repent of."

This was no time for personal opinion, preaching, murmuring, war cries or goofing off. Just holy, orderly silence. The first day must have seemed like a waste of time and energy to some. Yet much was accomplished. They were obedient to God's every instruction! No one added to or took away from God's plan. "Has the Lord as great delight in burnt offerings and sacrifices, as in obeying the voice of the Lord? Behold, to obey is better than sacrifice..." (1 Sam. 15:22).

Further, in making the Israelites march around the city once each day for six days and seven times on the seventh day, it is obvious that the Lord was teaching His people not only obedience, but patience and timing. I've often wondered what was going on in the minds of the inhabitants of Jericho. Was God lulling them to sleep with a false sense of security? What would you think if all your enemies ever did was silently march around your fortress?

But it came to pass on the seventh day that they rose early, about the dawning of the day, and marched around the city seven times in the same manner. On that day only they marched around the city seven times. And the seventh time it was so, when the priests blew the trumpets, that Joshua said to the people: "Shout, for the Lord has given you the city!" (Josh. 6:15-16)

This was no ordinary shout! It had been bottled up in them for six days, faith and absolute obedience wanting desperately to express itself in victory. "By faith the walls of Jericho fell down after they were encircled for seven days" (Heb. 11:30). How much of our shouting at our city walls and gates are noise and not faith?

So the people shouted when the priests blew the trumpets. And it happened when the people heard the sound of the trumpet, and the people shouted with a great shout, that the wall fell down flat. Then the people went up into the city, every man straight before him, and they took the city (Josh. 6:20).

Then, and only then, was victory theirs for the taking. It was the culmination of a process of warfare involving commitment, cleansing and unconditional obedience. Let's summarize and glean a few truths from the taking of Jericho to apply in taking our own cities for God:

1) No city is too tough for God.

2) Gaze on your city through the eyes of faith.

3) Even though it is God who is doing the fighting, we still have our responsibilities.

4) Stay humble.

5) Use His Word and stay in His presence.

6) Survey the territory.

7) Stick to God's plan.

8) Even if you don't see instant results, keep the trumpets blowing.

9) Always remember, God is not slack concerning His promise; the walls will come down!

CHAPTER 5

Ai: Disobedience Brings Defeat

But the children of Israel committed a trespass regarding the accursed things, for Achan the son of Carmi, the son of Zabdi, the son of Zerah of the tribe of Judah, took of the accursed things; so the anger of the Lord burned against the children of Israel (Josh. 7:1).

One would think that if a city as strong as Jericho fell as it did, the next challenge would be a piece of cake, but sin was found in the camp. Success can, and too often has, blinded the eyes of many good Christian leaders who felt God would turn His back on their "little shortcomings" because they were doing so much for the kingdom. (Pride, fostered by a false sense of security, will always result in the undoing of the best of plans.) At the outset of the Ai campaign Joshua sticks to what worked well at Jericho.

Now Joshua sent men from Jericho to Ai, which is beside Beth Aven, on the east side of Bethel, and spoke to them, saying, "Go up and spy out the country." So the men went up and spied out Ai (Josh. 7:2).

But notice the inflated opinion of themselves! "We are now a great nation," they seemed to say, "and our dependency is on our own might."

And they returned to Joshua and said to him, "Do not let all the people go up, but let about two or three thousand men go up and attack Ai. Do not weary all the people there, for the people of Ai are few." So about three thousand men went up there from the people, but they fled before the men of Ai. And the men of Ai struck down about thirty-six men, for they chased them from before the gate as far as Shebarim, and struck them down on the descent; therefore the hearts of the people melted and became like water (Josh. 7:3-5).

We should never underestimate the enemy. Some small towns I've visited were as wicked and evil as large metropolitan areas. The real issue here is the "leavening of the whole lump." Satan doesn't need much to work with in resisting the advances of the church. One may now see why Ananias and Sapphira had to be removed from the early church. Satan moved on them to "lie to the Holy Ghost." If we who are commissioned to take our cities allow the Achans, Ananiases and Sapphiras to participate with us in battle, we will be fighting with the arm of the flesh and not by God's Spirit. The result will be only defeat, disgrace, sorrow and confusion.

Then Joshua tore his clothes, and fell to the earth on his face before the ark of the Lord until evening, both he and the elders of Israel; and they put dust on their heads. And Joshua said, "Alas, Lord God, why have You brought this people over the Jordan at all — to deliver us into the hand of the Amorites, to destroy us? Oh, that we had been content, and dwelt on the other side of the Jordan! O Lord, what shall I say when Israel turns its back before its enemies? For the Canaanites and all the inhabitants of the land will hear of it, and surround us, and cut off our name from the earth. Then what will You do for Your great name?" (Josh. 7:6-9)

Pastor friend, ever feel like this? "Why, God, have you sent me to this city to be salt and light and I'm getting my teeth kicked in? My congregation is fleeing from the enemy and our church has become a reproach."

It's amazing when we really get down to business with God how He reveals the problem.

So the Lord said to Joshua, "Get up! Why do you lie thus on your face? Israel has sinned, and they have also transgressed My covenant which I commanded them. For they have even taken some of the accursed things, and have both stolen and deceived; and they have also put it among their own stuff. Therefore the children of Israel could not stand before their enemies, but turned their backs before their enemies, because they have become doomed to destruction. Neither will I be with you anymore, unless you destroy the accursed from among you. Get up, sanctify the people, and say, 'Sanctify yourselves for tomorrow, because thus says the Lord God of Israel: "There is an accursed thing in your midst, O Israel; you cannot stand before your enemies until you take away the accursed thing from among you" ' " (Josh. 7:10-13).

Ai is taken!

Then the Lord said to Joshua: "Do not be afraid, nor be dismayed; take all the people of war with you, and arise, go up to Ai. See, I have given into your hand the king of Ai, his people, his city, and his land" (Josh. 8:1).

Once certain adjustments had taken place, such as the stoning of Achan (Josh. 7:25), the people of God were again in a city-taking mode.

The Lord's word "arise" to Joshua needs closer scrutiny. Joshua was obviously on his knees, seeking answers from Almighty God on where they missed it and how they could continue. He didn't confer with flesh and blood but with the One who has all the answers. The plan God has for you to take your city will come through revelation on your knees and in His presence!

A. W. Pink says, "The method by which Ai was to be taken was quite different from the one used against the first stronghold of the Canaanites, which shows us, among other things, that God does not work uniformly" (Gleanings from Joshua, The Quest of Ai, p. 211).

Even though today there are common denominators in impacting any city, such as prayer, fasting and power preaching, God still has a unique plan for every city which must come through divine inspiration. A pastor friend of mine down in Argentina said, "You Americans have a book and steps for every situation conceivable. You are very methodical and organized in your approach to ministry. We here in Argentina have only the Bible and the direction of the Holy Spirit." He really laughed when I told him I was there to research a new book on warfare. He was very kind to say, "Well if there is one area of lack, it's good teaching on city-taking."

I have to agree totally with my Argentine friend. No book, tape series or video will ever replace prayer and the reading of the Word. Books, like this one, are supplemental tools and that is all!

The method God chose is quite interesting.

> *And he commanded them, saying: "Behold, you shall lie in ambush against the city, behind the city. Do not go very far from the city, but all of you be ready. Then I and all the people who are with me will approach the city; and it will come about, when they come out against us at the first, that we shall flee before them. For they will come out after us till we have drawn them from the city, for they will say, 'They are fleeing before us as at the first.' Therefore we will flee before them. Then you shall rise from the ambush and seize the city, for the Lord your God will deliver it into your hand"* (Josh. 8:4-7).

Basically what He said was, "Set a trap by enticing the men of war to come out after you. You will appear undermanned, and since they whipped you the first time, they will feel very secure and over confident." We are not ignorant of Satan's devices (2 Cor. 2:11), and can use his own stratagems against him.

> *Then you shall rise from the ambush and seize the city...* (Josh. 8:7).

It may seem strange at first that our Almighty God would use such a tactic to defeat the enemy. Casual readers may shake their head in wonderment. Yet, take a long look at the plan of redemption. How our Father flushed Satan out! By overplaying his hand he crucified the Lord of Glory to his own undoing.

> *But we speak the wisdom of God in a mystery, the hidden wisdom which God ordained before the ages for our glory, which none of the rulers of the age knew; for had they known, they would not have crucified the Lord of Glory* (1 Cor. 2:7-8).

In our modern cities there are major and minor strongholds. Places of influence and control will be governmental, financial, philosophical, religious, or any other place that shapes and molds society to conform to the world. Satan's underlying strategy is to make man dependent on the system for standards, rules, provision, education, self-esteem, entertainment. Our commission is to turn men's hearts to God. For people to make a clear choice, they first must see clearly. Because our generation has shied away from absolutes, they are stumbling around in the dark not knowing good from evil, right from wrong. Like tender plants left unstaked, they grow wild, with absolutely no sense of direction. The believer, on the other hand, whose life is bound to the Word of God, grows straight and strong. More than once Jesus called the Pharisees, "Fools and blind guides, calling wrong right and right wrong!" One only has to look at the laws our nation has passed concerning abortion, homosexual rights, prayer in school, just to name a few, to see how successful Satan's strategy is. Our work is cut out for us, but the Lord promises to use and bless our efforts.

Thus says God the Lord, Who created the heavens and stretched them out, Who spread forth the earth and that which comes from it, Who gives breath to the people on it, And spirit to those who walk on it: "I, the Lord, have called You in righteousness, and will hold Your hand; I will keep You and give You as a covenant to the people, as a light to the Gentiles, To open blind eyes, to bring out prisoners from the prison, Those who sit in darkness from the prison house" (Is. 42:5-7).

I know the taste of discouragement, even despair, as I look at my city. At times, I feel like a sculptor using toothpicks and a plastic hammer to carve out a masterpiece from marble. But then I am reminded of the cities to which Paul was called. Corinth was one wild and woolly place. It's no great mystery why he was inspired to write what he did in 2 Corinthians 4:1-18:

Therefore, since we have this ministry, as we have received mercy, we do not lose heart. But we have renounced the hidden things of shame, not walking in craftiness nor handling the word of God deceitfully, but by manifestation of the truth commending ourselves to every man's conscience in the sight of God. But even if our gospel is veiled, it is veiled to those who are perishing, whose minds the god of this age has blinded, who do not believe, lest the light of the gospel of the glory of Christ, who is the image of God, should shine on them. For we do not preach ourselves, but Christ Jesus the Lord, and ourselves your servants for Jesus' sake. For it is the God who commanded light to shine out of darkness who has shone in our hearts to give the light of the knowledge of the glory of God in the face of Jesus Christ.

But we have this treasure in earthen vessels, that the excellence of the power may be of God and not of us. We are hard pressed on every side, yet not crushed; we are perplexed, but not in despair; persecuted, but not forsaken; struck down, but not destroyed, always carrying about the body the dying of the Lord Jesus, that the life of Jesus also may be manifested in our body. For we who live are always delivered to death for Jesus' sake, that the life of Jesus also may be manifested in our mortal flesh. So then death is working in us, but life in you.

But since we have the same spirit of faith, according to what is written, I believed and therefore I spoke, we also believe and therefore speak, knowing that He who raised up the Lord Jesus will also raise us up with Jesus, and will present us with you. For all things are for your sakes, that grace, having spread through the many, may cause thanksgiving to abound to the glory of God.

Therefore we do not lose heart. Even though our outward man is perishing, yet the inward man is being renewed day by day. For our light affliction, which is but for a moment, is working for us a far more exceeding and eternal weight of glory, while we do not look at the things which are seen, but at the things which are not seen. For the things which are seen are temporal, but the things which are not seen are eternal.

By attacking the strongholds of our cities through prayer, fasting, power-preaching, evangelism and activism, we will flush out the enemy. In his state of confusion and anger we can then "make men see" the difference between the two kingdoms. We declare that heaven or hell both demand decision, not chance. Any prisoner in his right mind who is given a legal chance for a full pardon will jump at the opportunity with very little prompting.

A city left open

Now it happened, when the king of Ai saw it, that the men of the city hastened and rose early and went out against Israel to battle, he and all his people, at an appointed place before the plain. But he did not know that there was an ambush against him behind the city. And Joshua and all Israel made as if they were beaten before them, and fled by the way of the wilderness. So all the people who were in Ai were called together to pursue them. And they pursued Joshua and were drawn away from the city. There was not a man left in Ai or Bethel who did not go out after Israel. So they left the city open and pursued Israel.

Then the Lord said to Joshua, "Stretch out the spear that is in your hand toward Ai, for I will give it into your hand." And Joshua stretched out the spear that he had in his hand toward the city. So those in ambush arose quickly out of their place; they ran as soon as he had stretched out his hand, and they entered the city and took it, and hastened to set the city on fire. And when the men of Ai looked behind them, they saw, and behold, the smoke of the city ascended to heaven. So they had no power to flee this way or that way, and the people who had fled to the wilderness turned back on the pursuers (Josh. 8:14-20).

What is needed today is that the spiritual leaders, like Joshua, stretch out the spear toward our cities so that the people of God may arise quickly and take control. Pink puts the situation in perspective:

The land of Canaan had already been conquered, so far as its standing armies had been completely routed, its principal strongholds destroyed, and its kings slain. Yet much of its

39

actual territory was still in the hands of its original inhabitants, who remained to be dispossessed. It is important to distinguish between the work which had been done by Joshua and that which still remained for Israel to do. He had overthrown the ruling powers, captured their forts, and subdued the Canaanites to such an extent as had given Israel firm foothold in the country. But he had not exterminated the population in every portion of it, yea, powerful nations still dwelt in parts thereof, as is clear from Judges 2:20-23, and Judges 3:1-4; so that much was still demanded from Israel. Therein we behold again the accuracy of the type. The anti-typical Joshua has secured for His people an inalienable title to the heavenly Canaan, yet formidable foes have to be overcome and much hard fighting done by them before they enter into their eternal rest. The same is true of the present enjoyment thereof: faith and hope encounter much opposition ere there is an experiential participation of the goodly heritage which Christ has obtained for them. (A. W. Pink, *Gleanings from Joshua*, The Division of the Land, Moody Press, p. 335).

Lessons from Ai

We can learn many valuable spiritual principles by studying God's strategy at Ai:

1) Revival may not happen in your city exactly the way it did in another.

2) A small town doesn't always mean little resistance.

3) Don't get discouraged if you've been pushed back a time or two.

4) Get your battle plan on your knees.

5) The plan may seem a bit bizarre at first.

6) Flush the enemies out so that all can see them for what they are.

7) When the city opens, act quickly.

CHAPTER 6

Ziklag: Pursuit and Recovery

Now it happened, when David and his men came to Ziklag, on the third day, that the Amalekites had invaded the South and Ziklag and burned it with fire, and had taken captive the women and those who were there, from small to great; they did not kill anyone, but carried them away and went their way. So David and his men came to the city, and there it was, burned with fire; and their wives, their sons, and their daughters had been taken captive (1 Sam. 30:1-3).

The greatest danger to our nation is the breakup of the family unit. A recent article I read in the San Francisco Examiner predicted that two-thirds of all first-time marriages across the nation will end in divorce. I thought, Dear God, what about California? Satan has made the modern marriage a paper covenant, easy to destroy.

To survive in the Bay Area, the bread winner has to win a lot of bread. Long, stressful hours at the office, irritating commutes, pressure to keep pace with the Joneses — all this has resulted in neglected women and children who have been taken captive by the enemy. Wives today are so depressed and confused. We men can't understand why they aren't happy. We work all day to provide them a good home, car, clothes, food, a little fun now and then. Isn't that enough?

Recently, Carla and I were hosting Trinity Broadcasting Network's "Praise the Lord" program and one of our guests was my friend, Ed Silvoso. On the plane back to San Jose we were discussing this very subject. Ed said, "It is no wonder the Bible tells us to live with our wives in understanding, giving honor to them" (1 Pet. 3:7). He went on to say, "Personally, I don't understand the way a woman perceives time and money. 'I'll only be a minute, dear,' or, 'But, honey, I saved you $400 on this wonderful sale.' " His favorite was, "I don't have a thing to wear," when the closet appears full of nice clothes. I poked my wife, Carla, in the ribs as Ed continued. God had to teach me how to read and understand my wife, and how to listen. What seems like a small, trivial matter to us men is a big deal to our wives. The main problem with us guys is that we don't listen. We observe. Perhaps that is why God tells women that the best way to win a point is not by arguing but with "chaste conduct."

Carla reminds me, "Honey, I don't want all your time, just some quality time." With a little tender maintenance we can keep our wives from being taken captive by spirits of divorce, rejection, depression, suicide and lust. On the other hand, the Bible tells the wives to submit to and respect us men. We need it. We are accomplishment oriented. As Dr. Ed Cole says, "We are headlines, while our wives are fine print." We desperately need the approval of our wives to tell us we are doing a good job as providers. Affirmation will enhance affection, communication, and sex, as well as keep the enemy at bay!

In the story in 1 Samuel 30 the enemy came while the men were away. David and his men wept bitterly before the Lord. It's a horrible revelation to know your family is gone. Years ago, I was on a trout fishing trip with a friend up in the High Sierras. When I dropped him off at his house it was completely empty. His wife had moved out lock, stock, and barrel. My friend was crushed!

As we read in verse 6, the spirit of anger usually accompanies grief and despair. When deep hurt hits a family, my how the accusations start flying! Our old enemy uses the same bag of tricks on all of us.

...But David strengthened himself in the Lord his God! (1 Sam. 30:6)

By doing this he received instruction. "Pursue, for you shall surely overtake them and without fail recover all" (1 Sam. 30:8). If we are willing to fight for our cities, we must first fight for our own families. All of David's men were not strong enough to fight. Two hundred, or one-third of them, were too weak to cross the Brook Besor (1 Sam. 30:9). Some of our brothers and sisters today are so war-weary and beaten down they must stay back and let the strong press on for them.

Again, we see the Lord bringing assistance from a strange source — an Egyptian, a servant of an Amalekite who dumped him because he was sick and had become a liability. Sounds like the devil, doesn't it? I know beyond any doubt that many of Satan's chief servants in our cities will soon end up being some of our strongest allies, for we will give them meat and drink that will satisfy their souls.

And David said to him, "Can you take me down to this troop?" And he said, "Swear to me by God that you will neither kill me nor deliver me into the hands of my master, and I will take you down to this troop." So when he had brought him down, there they were, spread out over all the land, eating and drinking and dancing, because of all the great spoil which they had taken from the land of the Philistines and from the land of Judah. And David attacked them from twilight until the evening of the next day. Not a man of them escaped, except four hundred young men who rode on camels and fled. So David recovered all that the Amalekites had carried away, and David rescued his two wives. And nothing of theirs was lacking, either small or great, sons or daughters, spoil or anything which they had taken from them; David recovered all (1 Sam. 30:15-19).

I'm sure David and his men were weary from the pursuit, but the hope of getting their families back gave them strength.

This story had a strange twist that reveals a truth we can't ignore. Great victories can at times bring pride to those who forget who really did the fighting. Attitudes can become haughty and a spirit of self-righteousness can take over if we're not guarded.

Lessons from Ziklag

1. Do not neglect the family.
2. Satan preys on the minds of lonely wives and children.
3. Men need respect, women understanding.
4. Spiritual warfare begins at home.
5. Fight fearlessly for your family.
6. Don't settle for second best; recover all!

CHAPTER 7

Jerusalem: Citadel of Compromise

> *Then all the tribes of Israel came to David at Hebron and spoke, saying, "Indeed we are your bone and your flesh. Also, in time past, when Saul was king over us, you were the one who led Israel out and brought them in; and the Lord said to you, 'You shall shepherd My people Israel, and be ruler over Israel.'" So all the elders of Israel came to the king at Hebron, and King David made a covenant with them at Hebron before the Lord. And they anointed David king over Israel. David was thirty years old when he began to reign, and he reigned forty years. In Hebron he reigned over Judah seven years and six months, and in Jerusalem he reigned thirty-three years over all Israel and Judah. And the king of his men went to Jerusalem against the Jebusites, the inhabitants of the land, who spoke to David, saying, "You shall not come in here; but the blind and the lame will repel you," thinking, David cannot come in here. Nevertheless David took the stronghold of Zion (that is, the City of David) (2 Sam. 5:1-7).*

It would behoove us to closely inspect the taking of this planet's most famous city, Jerusalem, by David and his mighty men. My dear friend, Dr. Lester Sumrall wrote a book entitled, *Jerusalem, Where Empires Die*, which I highly recommend. The account of David wrestling the stronghold of Zion out of the hands of the ungodly Canaanites is brief but full of importance. The taking of Jerusalem is David's first recorded feat after all the tribes of Israel had anointed him king. Up until then only Judah recognized the hand of God on David (2 Sam. 2:4). The other tribes who should have welcomed a change of kings fiercely fought against God's will and insisted on having Saul's son, Ishbosheth, as their leader. Yet, seven and a half years later they confessed that they knew all along that David was the one God had destined to be the deliverer of Israel.

Also, in time past, when Saul was king over us, you were the one who led Israel out and brought them in; and the Lord said to you, "You shall shepherd My people Israel, and be ruler over Israel" (2 Sam. 5:2).

It is both amazing and saddening to see how true this still is today. Professing Christians who recognize anything except their own fleshly desires and that which gratifies their own self-interest, "kicking against the goads," while yet pursuing fabricated visions and dreams. How patient God must be with all of us!

But, in spite of man, God always fulfills His purpose. The rebels submit to David and are ready for new orders. "Indeed we are your bone and your flesh" (2 Sam. 5:1). David's power has grown beyond mere numbers. He has their hearts. Their conversion, if you will, is complete. We have a new leader and we are one with him!

We read in the New Testament, "But he who is joined to the Lord is one spirit with Him" (1 Cor. 6:17). A church that is torn by strife and confusion is no threat to the enemy, but a united congregation with a warring spirit can do much damage to the kingdom of darkness. God Himself acknowledges the force of togetherness. "And the Lord said, 'Indeed the people are one and they all have one language, and this is what they begin to do; now nothing that they propose to do will be withheld from them'" (Gen. 11:6).

Let's size up David's situation. The mighty fortress of Zion is in the hands of the Jebusites. Why? How did this evil lot gain control of such a strategic city? The book of Joshua gives us the answer and a warning as well.

After the death of Moses the servant of the Lord, it came to pass that the Lord spoke to Joshua the son of Nun, Moses' assistant, saying: "Moses My servant is dead. Now therefore, arise, go over this Jordan, you and all this people, to the land which I am giving them — the children of Israel. Every place that the sole of your foot will tread upon I have given you, as I said to Moses. From the wilderness and this Lebanon as far as the great river, the River Euphrates, all the land of the Hittites, and to the Great Sea toward the going down of the sun, shall be your territory. No man shall be able to stand before you all the days of your life; as I was with Moses, so I will be with you. I will not leave you nor forsake you. Be strong and of good courage, for to this people you shall divide as an inheritance the land which I swore to their fathers to give them" (Josh. 1:1-6).

So Joshua said to the children of Israel, "Come here, and hear the words of the Lord your God." And Joshua said, "By this you shall know that the living God is among you, and that He will without fail drive out from before you the Canaanites and the Hittites and the Hivites and the Perizzites and the Girgashites and the Amorites and the Jebusites" (Josh.3:9-10).

Over and over again God commanded the children of Israel to drive out completely the enemies of God from the land He promised them. With his dying breath, Joshua once again rehearses God's command.

For the Lord has driven out from before you great and strong nations; but as for you, no one has been able to stand against you to this day. One man of you shall chase a thousand, for the Lord your God is He who fights for you, as He has promised you. Therefore take diligent heed to yourselves, that you love the Lord your God. Or else, if indeed you do go back, and cling to the remnant of these nations — these that remain among you — and make marriages with them, and go in to them and they to you, know for certain that the Lord your God will no longer drive out these nations from before you. But they shall be snares and traps to you, and scourges on your sides and thorns in your eyes, until you perish from this good land which the Lord your God has given you (Josh. 23:9-13).

The tribe of Judah had already failed in their attempt to rid Jerusalem of the Jebusites. "As for the Jebusites, the inhabitants of Jerusalem, the children of Judah could not drive them out; but the Jebusites dwell with the children of Judah at Jerusalem to this day" (Josh. 15:63); and Joshua knew there would be consequences. Likewise, the children of Benjamin fell into the same trap. "But the children of Benjamin did not drive out the Jebusites who inhabited Jerusalem; so the Jebusites dwell with the children of Benjamin in Jerusalem to this day" (Judg. 1:21).

How foolish it is for us to think we can compromise God's commands and get away with it! It's as though some believe God Almighty has become senile or forgetful with age. Many think His mercy and grace are a license for disobedience. Our sins always catch up with us and, yes, we will reap what we sow. Note carefully the force of the next passage:

> Then the Angel of the Lord came up from Gilgal to Bochim, and said: "I led you up from Egypt and brought you to the land of which I swore to your fathers; and I said, 'I will never break My covenant with you. And you shall make no covenant with the inhabitants of this land; you shall tear down their altars.' But you have not obeyed My voice. Why have you done this? Therefore I also said, 'I will not drive them out before you; but they shall be thorns in your side, and their gods shall be a snare to you.' " And so it was when the Angel of the Lord spoke these words to all the children of Israel, that the people lifted up their voice and wept (Judg. 2:1-4).

David had a mess on his hands because his forefathers settled for second best. Today you and I are up against strongholds unprecedented in America's history because we decided to live with ungodliness instead of crushing it. Humanism, abortion, sodomy, crime, greed—all have fortified themselves and in some cases legalized themselves against those who still fight for righteousness. But let us take courage, for when the enemies of God are the most confident of their strength, their demise is most imminent. God still has a few water shafts into our cities, and daily mighty men and women are enlisting with us to take back our cities.

And the king and his men went to Jerusalem against the Jebusites, the inhabitants of the land, who spoke to David, saying, "You shall not come in here; but the blind and the lame will repel you," thinking, David cannot come in here. Nevertheless David took the stronghold of Zion (that is the City of David). Now David said on that day, "Whoever climbs up by way of the water shaft and defeats the Jebusites (the lame and the blind, who are hated by David's soul), he shall be chief and captain." Therefore they say, "The blind and the lame shall not come into the house." So David dwelt in the stronghold, and called it the City of David. Then David built all around from the Millo and inward. So David went on and became great, and the Lord God of hosts was with him (2 Sam. 5:6-10).

A fascinating side note is found in verse 11.

Then Hiram king of Tyre sent messengers to David, and cedar trees, and carpenters and masons. And they built David a house.

After David subdued and captured Zion, he finds favor with a Gentile king who wants to bless him. There are Hirams all over our cities who once they see us pushing back the modern-day Jebusites will also come to bless us.

Lessons from Jerusalem

1. Unity and purpose are essential in city taking.
2. Numbers are not as important as the strength of faith.
3. Church people are looking for strong, anointed, believable leaders to follow.
4. The right cause always rallies the troops.
5. God has an entrance into your city, one the enemy doesn't know about.

CHAPTER 8

Samaria: A City Twice Visited

The woman then left her waterpot, went her way into the city, and said to the men, "Come, see a Man who told me all things that I ever did. Could this be the Christ?" Then they went out of the city and came to Him (Jn. 4:28-30).

The first forty-two verses of the fourth chapter of John are a stimulating picture of what this book is all about. They focus on Samaria's first visitation.

So He came to a city of Samaria which is called Sychar, near the plot of ground that Jacob gave to his son Joseph. Now Jacob's well was there. Jesus therefore, being wearied from His journey, sat thus by the well. It was about the sixth hour. A woman of Samaria came to draw water. Jesus said to her, "Give Me a drink." For His disciples had gone away into the city to buy food. Then the woman of Samaria said to Him, "How is it that You, being a Jew, ask a drink from me, a Samaritan woman?" For Jews have no dealings with Samaritans. Jesus answered and said to her, "If you knew the gift of God, and who it is who says to you, 'Give Me a drink,' you would have asked Him, and He would have given you living water." The woman said to Him, "Sir, You have nothing to draw with, and the well is deep. Where then do You get that living water? Are You greater than our father Jacob, who gave us the well, and drank from it himself, as well as his sons and his livestock?" Jesus answered and said to her, "Whoever drinks of this water will thirst again, but whoever drinks of the water that I shall give him will never thirst. But the water that I shall give him will become in him a fountain of water springing up into everlasting life." The woman said to Him, "Sir, give me this water, that I may not thirst, nor come here to draw." Jesus said to her, "Go, call your husband, and come here." The woman answered and said, "I have no husband." Jesus said to her, "You have well said, I have no husband, for you have had five husbands, and the one whom you now have is not your husband; in that you spoke truly." The woman said to Him, "Sir, I perceive that You are a prophet. Our fathers worshiped on this mountain, and you Jews say that in Jerusalem is the place where one ought to worship." Jesus said to her, "Woman, believe Me, the hour is coming when you will neither on this mountain, nor in Jerusalem worship the Father. You worship what you do not know; we know what we worship, for salvation is of the Jews. But the hour is coming, and now is, when the true worshipers will worship the Father in spirit and truth; for the Father is seeking such to worship Him. God is Spirit, and those who worship Him must worship in spirit and truth." The woman said to Him, "I know that Messiah is coming (who is called Christ). When He comes, He will tell us all things." Jesus said to her, "I who speak to you am He."

And at this point His disciples came, and they marveled that He talked with a woman; yet no one said, "What do You seek?" or, "Why are You talking with her?" The woman then left her waterpot, went her way into the city, and said to the men, "Come see a Man who told me all things that I ever did. Could this be the Christ?" Then they went out to the city and came to Him (Jn. 4:5-30).

The next passage focuses on Samaria's second visitation.

Then Philip went down to the city of Samaria and preached Christ to them. And the multitudes with one accord heeded the things spoken by Philip, hearing and seeing the miracles which he did. For unclean spirits, crying with a loud voice, came out of many who were possessed; and many who were paralyzed and lame were healed. And there was great joy in that city (Acts 8:5-8).

Before we consider what happened in Samaria, we need to know who the Samaritans were. The Samaritans were mongrel Jews both in blood and religion. The deep resentment the Jews felt for the Samaritans went back several centuries. When the Assyrians conquered Samaria, the capital of the Northern Kingdom, in 721 B.C., they deported the local population and imported alien nations to resettle the area. These peoples brought their own idolatrous pagan religions with them and were later instructed in the worship of Jehovah. What resulted was a curious blending of Jehovah worship mixed with idolatry, as described in 2 Kings 17:28-41:

Then one of the priests whom they had carried away from Samaria came and dwelt in Bethel, and taught them how they should fear the Lord.

However every nation continued to make gods of its own, and put them in the houses of the high places which the Samaritans had made, every nation in the cities where they dwelt. The men of Babylon made Succoth Benoth, the men of Cuth made Nergal, the men of Hamath made Ashima, and the Avites made Nibhaz and Tartak; and the Sepharvites burned their children in fire to Adrammelech and Anammelech, the gods of Sepharvaim. So they feared the Lord, and from every class they appointed for themselves priests of the high places, who sacrificed for them in the shrines of the high places. They feared the Lord, yet served their own gods —according to the rituals of the nations from among whom they were carried away. To this day they continued practicing the former rituals; they do not fear the Lord, nor do they follow their statutes or their ordinances, or the law and commandment which the Lord had commanded the children of Jacob, whom He named Israel, with whom the Lord had made a covenant and charged them, saying: "You shall not fear other gods, nor bow down to them to serve them nor sacrifice to them; but the Lord, who brought you up from the land of Egypt with great power and an outstretched arm, Him you shall fear, Him you shall worship, and to Him you shall offer sacrifice. And the statutes, the ordinances, the law, and the commandment which He wrote to you, you shall be careful to observe forever; you shall not fear other gods. And the covenant that I have made with you, you shall not forget, nor shall you fear other gods. But the Lord your God you shall fear; and He will deliver you from the hand of all your enemies." However they did not obey, but they followed their former rituals. So these nations feared the Lord, yet served their carved images; also their children and their children's children have continued doing as their fathers did, even to this day.

H. R. Reynolds in his exposition from The Pulpit Commentary, The Gospel According to St. John, p. 159, explains the deepening antagonism between the Jews and the Samaritans:

In the time of Ezra and Nehemiah, efforts on their (Samaritans) part to share in the honours and independence of Judah were sternly interdicted, and the interdict avenged by angry recriminations which delayed the progress of reconstruction. The antagonism commenced then was deepened into a deadly rivalry by the erection of a temple to Jehovah on Mount Gerizim (B.C. 409), and by Manasseh, brother of the high priest of Judah, being driven from Jerusalem by his refusal to renounce Sanballat's daughter, and by his becoming high priest of the heretical temple. This temple in Gerizim, in close proximity with the site on Shechem, the abode of the first patriarchs, gave dignity and solidity to some of their traditions and claims; and the modifications they had introduced into the text of the Pentateuch in their celebrated version of it helped to aggravate the schism between the two peoples...

Samaritan hatred of the Jews led them to purchase peace during the cruel oppression of Judah under Antiochus Epiphanes by dedicating their temple to Zeus (Josephus, 'Ant,' xii 5, 5) and again by siding with the Syrians against the Maccabees.

So you see there was no love loss between the Jews and the Samaritans. This makes John 4:4 fascinating. "But He needed to go through Samaria." According to Jewish custom, He could have crossed the Jordan and passed through Peraea instead, a bit out of the way but feasible. I believe the "need" was a prompting of the Holy Spirit. We must never forget we are commissioned to go into all the world, even despicable, hostile places. Later, Christ would command, "But you shall receive power when the Holy Spirit has come upon you; and you shall be witnesses to Me in Jerusalem, and in all Judea and Samaria, and to the end of the earth" (Acts 1:8). This seems inconsistent with His treatment of the Samaritans in Matthew 10:5: "...Do not go into the way of the Gentiles, and do not enter a city of the Samaritans."

Once again Reynolds notes:

Still, there is a difference between Christ's passing through Samaria on His way to Galilee, and his limiting the early proclamation of the kingdom to the lost sheep of the house of Israel. The disciples were not then to be entrusted with a commission which, not until after Pentecost they would fulfill with so much joy (The Pulpit Commentary, The Gospel According to St. John, p.159).

Understanding the deep-seated animosity between Jew and Samaritan, we can make more sense of the woman's question in vs. 9: "Then the woman of Samaria said to Him, 'How is it that You, being a Jew, ask a drink from me, a Samaritan woman?' For Jews have no dealings with Samaritans" (Jn. 4:9). Jesus simply ignores her objection to the feud between the Jews and the Samaritans. He moves in immediately with divine instruction. Some issues are best left alone. To quote Matthew Henry, "Quarrels about religion are usually the most implacable of all quarrels."

The woman's answer is laced with scorn. "Who do you think you are?" she seems to be saying to this stranger. But she does call Him, "sir," so perhaps this peasant girl caught a glimpse of glory in our Lord. Jesus has laid the bait and now is ready to set the hook. With a word of knowledge her scandalous past is exposed, not to embarrass her, but to bring conviction to her conscience. How wonderful are God's gifts. A few words under the guidance of the Holy Spirit can do far more than hours of the finest sermonizing.

After acknowledging Him as a prophet and receiving a mini-sermon on true worship, she heads for the heart of the city to tell the men, "Come, see a Man who told me all things that I ever did. Could this be the Christ?" (Jn. 4:29) A revival breaks out in the city. "And many of the Samaritans of that city believed in Him because of the word of the woman who testified, 'He told me all that I ever did' " (Jn. 4:39). One preacher and one lonely woman impact a whole city!

Three years later the same region is again visited by God, this time through a deacon-turned-evangelist, named Philip. We need to understand the events leading up to Philip's visit to Samaria. With the martyrdom of Stephen came a fury of violence against the early church. The persecutors, tasting blood and in a feeding frenzy, were led by a young Pharisee named Saul of Tarsus.

Of this intense persecution, Matthew Henry writes:

> *What was the effect of this persecution? They were all scattered abroad, not all the believers, but all the preachers who were principally struck at, and against whom warrants were issued out to take them up. They, remembering our Master's rule (when they persecute you in one city, flee to another), dispersed themselves by agreement throughout the regions of Judea and of Samaria; not so much for fear of sufferings, (for Judea and Samaria were not so far off from Jerusalem but that if they made a public appearance there, as they determined to do, their persecutors' power would soon reach them there), but because they looked upon this as an intimation of Providence to them to scatter* (Matthew Henry's Commentary, The Acts, Vol. VI, pgs. 95-96).

So Philip's going down to Samaria was by design not chance. A preacher friend of mine once told me that persecution was God's way of keeping His remnant pure and holy. Without it we would flirt with tradition and compromise and become infected.

This city-wide revival came through the simplicity of preaching Christ. A minister's duty is to preach Jesus Christ, and Him crucified and glorified! The proof of Philip's preaching was the miracles. The citizens of Samaria needed little convincing when they saw heaven's blessing on Philip. They "heard" and they "saw." This brought "great joy in that city."

How absolutely insane it is for ministers across our land to pray for revival and yet from their pulpits to deny the gifts of the Spirit and their importance today! Through our Lord, a word of knowledge shook Samaria. With Philip it was signs and wonders, the casting out of demons and healing the sick. Our seminary students are told what they need is a Ph.D. in Biblical Studies to attract the masses. We are told to sharpen our pulpit skills with higher education and to saturate our messages with seventy-five dollar words! I am not against education or a minister bettering himself. Hopefully, I am gaining knowledge and wisdom daily. But like Paul we must never trust in human wisdom.

And I, brethren, when I came to you, did not come with excellence of speech or of wisdom declaring to you the testimony of God. For I determined not to know anything among you except Jesus Christ and Him crucified. I was with you in weakness, in fear, and in much trembling. And my speech and my preaching were not with persuasive words of human wisdom, but in demonstration of the Spirit and of power, that your faith should not be in the wisdom of men but in the power of God (1 Cor. 2:1-5).

Paul never let his education interfere with learning the ways of God.

Lessons from Samaria

1. God loves unloveable cities.
2. Many major third-world cities and nations will come to Jesus only if they see His works.
3. The gifts of the Spirit are absolutely necessary.
4. Reach the key people and they will reach their city.

CHAPTER 9

Ephesus: No City Too Tough for God!

Larry Huggins, a minister friend who pastors in San Francisco, opened a Sunday night service at our church a few years ago by asking the congregation a question. "I am going to describe a city of great importance to you and want to see if you can guess which one it is." Pastor Huggins proceeded in a serious tone of voice, "This city is located on the West Coast of a great nation. It's a very liberal city well known for its arts, beauty, excitement. A melting pot of various ethnic groups, this city is notorious for its luxury and licentiousness. Sorcery and magic are exceedingly common. The city is a center of commerce, with its ships flying flags from all over the world as they come and go out of the bay. The main worship of the city could be called, idolatrous or "New Age." He proceeded to ask, "What city am I talking about?" In unison the congregation roared, "San Francisco!" "No, Ephesus!" the grinning man of God proudly replied, knowing he had their full attention. The pastor went on to compare the striking similarities of ancient Ephesus and modern San Francisco. Even the latitude is remarkably close. Put your finger on a globe where San Francisco is and spin it around and see if you don't cross Ephesus.

The point that brother Huggins made that night which struck home to me was that if one little preacher named Paul with a handful of new converts, whom he immediately led into the fullness of the Holy Ghost (Acts 19:6), to make sure they were up to the task of impacting a wicked city! — if they could shock a major city, why can't San Francisco be taken also?

Paul taught in "the synagogue and spoke boldly for three months, reasoning and persuading concerning the things of the Kingdom of God" (Acts 19:8). He remained in Ephesus for two years and did mighty, yet unusual works. Again, his ministry in Ephesus reflects the same pattern we mentioned previously, the casting out of devils and the healing of the sick (vs. 12). Paul knew that words, as eloquent as they might be, were not enough to uproot idolatry and the worship of Diana. The working of miracles at Ephesus spoke loudly against the superstitions of the inhabitants. Magic, sorcery and the occult are never a match for the power of Almighty God.

And many who had believed came confessing and telling their deeds. Also, many of those who had practiced magic brought their books together and burned them in the sight of all. And they counted up the value of them, and it totaled fifty thousand pieces of silver. So the word of the Lord grew mightily and prevailed (Acts 19:18-20).

There is no city too hard for God if God's people will do what our wonderful Lord commanded them to do. "Most assuredly I say to you, he who believes in Me, the works that I do he will do also; and greater works than these he will do, because I go to My father" (Jn. 14:12).

Lessons from Ephesus

1. God enjoys moving where there is darkness (Gen. 1:2).
2. Look for revival in the world's most wicked cities.
3. Pray for boldness daily.
4. Strongly encourage the baptism of the Holy Ghost to all believers.
5. Challenge superstition publicly.

CHAPTER 10

Philippi: Epitome
of the Gentile World

Another unlikely city in which Christianity should find a foothold was Philippi, a Roman colony made up of Italians, Greeks and, of course, Macedonians. It was a military outpost fashioned after the great imperial city of Rome. There was no synagogue, only a place of prayer by the riverside (Acts 16:13). God always seems to have someone, somewhere praying for their region. Paul's desire was to go to Asia (Asia Minor), but the sacred control of an overruling God directed otherwise.

I look back at my coming to San Jose to pioneer a church and at the bizarre events which led my wife and me to a city in which I never would have dreamed I would be pastoring! People told us that they had prayed for years for someone like us to come to San Jose. One lady said that she saw me in a dream years before and that the Lord told her I would be her pastor. It's an awesome thing to be in the hands of the living God!

The events recorded in Acts 16:11-40 are hardly found in any modern manuals on how to start a successful church as a light-house to a city, yet our two heroes, Paul and Silas, simply went with the flow even when it meant rough sledding. Things seem to get off to a good start. They found a worshipper of God named Lydia, a wealthy businesswoman who dealt in purple dyes. The Lord opened her heart to the teachings of Paul, and she and her household were all baptized. What happened immediately after that is a good lesson for all believers. The devil and his kind are not always easily recognizable as some would teach.

Now it happened, as we went to prayer, that a certain slave girl possessed with a spirit of divination met us, who brought her masters much profit by fortune-telling. This girl followed Paul and us, and cried out, saying, "These men are the servants of the Most High God, who proclaim to us the way of salvation." And this she did for many days. But Paul, greatly annoyed, turned and said to the spirit, "I command you in the name of Jesus Christ to come out of her." And he came out that very hour (Acts 16:16-18).

Here's a little damsel following after Paul and his troop, crying out, "These men are the servants of the Most High God, who proclaimed to us the way of salvation" (vs. 17). Saying what is true with a hidden agenda or motive can be as damaging, if not more so, than an out-and-out lie. The devil enjoys a fabricated association with the things of God. To him it lends credibility to his devices, and unfortunately the ignorant buy into it. But here the devil mixes truth with lies. We are commanded to have no fellowship with darkness. Truth needs no help!

The deliverance of the slave girl from the spirit of divination (or python) didn't exactly bring a city-wide revival but instead got our two soldiers of the cross thrown into jail.

But when her masters saw that their hope of profit was gone, they seized Paul and Silas and dragged them into the marketplace to the authorities. And they brought them to the magistrates, and said, "These men, being Jews, exceedingly trouble our city; and they teach customs which are not lawful for us, being Romans, to receive or observe." Then the multitude rose up together against them; and the magistrates tore off their clothes and commanded them to be beaten with rods. And when they had laid many stripes on them, they threw them into prison, commanding the jailer to keep them securely (Acts 16:19-23).

Now Paul and Silas could have become discouraged and even angry with God for sending them there but, no, they began to sing in the dark. God answers with an earthquake! The jailer is gloriously saved, along with his whole household.

Then they spoke the word of the Lord to him and to all who were in his house. And he took them the same hour of the night and washed their stripes. And immediately he and all his family were baptized. Now when he had brought them into his house, he set food before them; and he rejoiced, having believed in God with all his household (Acts 16: 32-34).

Now we have Lydia, a Philippian jailer and a new church which will impact the city!

Lessons from Philippi

1. God will have the right people go to the right city.
2. Thank God for godly women.
3. Demons will tell the truth if it is to their advantage.
4. Keep singing in the dark.
5. God will shake us free.

CHAPTER 11

Authority!

Then Jesus came and spoke to them, saying, "All authority has been given to Me in heaven and on earth. Go therefore and make disciples of all the nations, baptizing them in the name of the Father and of the Son and of the Holy Spirit, teaching them to observe all things that I have commanded you; and lo I am with you always, even to the end of the age. Amen!" (Mt. 28:18-20).

One of the most important, if not the most important teaching to come out of the 70's was "the authority of the believer." As a young evangelical back then, my posture was the traditional belief that whatever happens must be the will of God and that we believers have little to say about anything. Satan was seldom mentioned, and no one spoke of demons. Blessing and calamity were both attributed to God Almighty as if one was not to know His ways.

We were told from the pulpit that the Lord has said, "For my thoughts are not your thoughts, nor are your ways my ways," (Is. 55:8). This was often quoted when the minister of our church was up against a tough situation like a death of a young person or some other unfortunate situation. We would all shake our dumb, ignorant heads up and down in agreement like good little sheep. And, of course, the mysteries of our omnipotent God were not to be questioned but accepted as wisdom from on high. This thinking made Christianity much more comfortable, with very little responsibility for the believer except church attendance and giving. Maybe a little participation but certainly no pressure. People might be offended. Why strive for ever-increasing faith when all is predestinated? Why buy concordances and study when it's all too ethereal and esoteric to understand? But, one day a real Bible teacher opened my eyes to truth. "In Isaiah," he said, "God is not talking to the saint who is working with Him but to the evil doer and the unrighteous man."

> Seek the Lord while He may be found, call upon Him while He is near. Let the wicked forsake his way, and the unrighteous man his thoughts; Let him return to the Lord, and He will have mercy on him; And to our God, for He will abundantly pardon. "For my thoughts are not your thoughts, nor are your ways My ways," says the Lord. "For as the heavens are higher than the earth, so are My ways higher than your ways, and my thoughts than your thoughts" (Is. 55:6-9).

As far as the mysteries of God go, Paul plainly states,

> In Him we have redemption through His blood, the forgiveness of sins, according to the riches of His grace which He made to abound toward us in all wisdom and prudence, having made known to us the mystery of His will, according to His good pleasure which He purposed in Himself, that in the dispensation of the fullness of the times He might gather together in one all things in Christ, both which are in heaven and which are on earth — in Him (Eph. 1:7-10).

Further, he says,

> For this reason I, Paul, the prisoner of Jesus Christ for you Gentiles — if indeed you have heard of the dispensation of the grace of God which was given to me for you, how that by revelation He made known to me the mystery (as I wrote before in a few words, by which, when you read, you may understand my knowledge in the mystery of Christ), which in other ages was not made known to the sons of men, as it has now been revealed by the Spirit to His holy apostles and prophets: that the Gentiles should be fellow heirs, of the same body, and partakers of His promise in Christ through the gospel, of which I became a minister according to the gift of

the grace of God given to me by the effective working of His power (Eph. 3:1-7).

Again, in Colossians he writes,

I now rejoice in my sufferings for you, and fill up in the flesh what is lacking in the afflictions of Christ, for the sake of His body, which is the church, of which I became a minister according to the stewardship from God which was given to me for you, to fulfill the word of God, the mystery which has been hidden from ages and from generations, but now has been revealed to His saints. To them God willed to make known what are the riches of the glory of this mystery among the Gentiles: which is Christ in you, the hope of glory (Col. 1:24-27).

If the will of God is still a mystery to you, it's certainly not the fault of our Lord! The Word of God is His will, and His will is for you and me to exercise our authority over principalities and dark powers. Our Lord indicated this the first time He sent His troops out to minister.

Then He called His twelve disciples together and gave them power and authority over all demons, and to cure diseases. He sent them to preach the kingdom of God and to heal the sick. And He said to them, "Take nothing for the journey, neither staffs nor bag nor bread nor money; and do not have two tunics apiece. Whatever house you enter, stay there, and from there depart. And whoever will not receive you, when you go out of that city, shake off the very dust from your feet as a testimony against them." So they departed and went through the towns, preaching the gospel and healing everywhere (Lk. 9:1-6).

Did you notice that the Scripture says He first gave them power and authority over all demons, then it mentions healing the sick and preaching the Word of the Kingdom. A chapter later He sends out "seventy others" to do the same, and when they returned the excitement of their victories is recorded in Luke 10:17:

Then the seventy returned with joy, saying, "Lord, even the demons are subject to us in Your name."

Jesus then responds:

... I saw Satan fall like lightning from heaven. Behold, I give you the authority to trample on serpents and scorpions, and over all the power of the enemy, and nothing shall by any means hurt you. Nevertheless do not rejoice in this, that the spirits are subject to you, but rather rejoice because your names are written in heaven (Lk. 10:18-20).

In His parting words to His disciples according to St. Mark we see once again an emphasis on the authority of those who proclaim the Good News.

And He said to them, "Go into all the world and preach the gospel to every creature. He who believes and is baptized will be saved; but he who does not believe will be condemned. And these signs will follow those who believe: In My name they will cast out demons; they will speak with new tongues; they will take up serpents; and if they drink anything deadly, it will by no means hurt them; they will lay hands on the sick, and they will recover" (Mk. 16:15-18).

After the resurrection, our Lord again drives home the point of power ministry.

But you shall receive power when the Holy Spirit has come upon you; and you shall be witnesses to Me in Jerusalem, and in all Judea and Samaria, and to the end of the earth (Acts 1:8).

It is obvious in reading the Acts of the Apostles that the early church had no problem with the Great Commission. Today it has been reduced to "waxing eloquent" from our prestigious pulpits, while our cities are going to hell. We are told that miracles, healings and the gifts are not for today. They served a purpose in the first century, but the civilized, educated world of today has no need for them. Talk about the blind leading the blind! To weaken Calvary's impact through human rationale is both sad and dangerous.

There has been, and I suppose always will be, the lunatic fringe who take truth and carry it over into the unpromised land of presumption. In this case, however, a little leaven doesn't spoil the whole lump. Because a few ignorant and misguided souls abuse the gifts and presume upon God's blessings is no cause to throw the baby out with the bath water when it comes to our God-given rights and privileges to stand up to Satan and his evil cadre and resist with the Word in Jesus' name!

The armor we wear is God's armor and is very recognizable to the spirit world. "Jesus I know and Paul I know..." (Acts 19:15). Can we all say we are known and feared by the demon world? I know my name is written in the Lamb's Book of Life, but I also pray Satan has my name written down as a man armed and dangerous.

Territorial Principalities

Recently my wife and I purchased a home in Morgan Hill, a small community a few miles south of San Jose. After being cooped up in a dinky condominium for far too long, we were naturally ecstatic to have our own place with room for our kids to run and play. Sarah and Jesse, our children, were excited as well. Not only would they have separate bedrooms, but their cats, Bear and Scamper, would have room to roam outside.

Two days after we moved in I was off to Argentina to preach and do research for this book. I called home a day after I arrived in Buenos Aires to check in and see how everyone was settling in. During our conversation, Carla remarked, "Oh, by the way, honey, pray for Bear. He has been missing since the morning you left." This was not like 'ol Bear. He was a black, long-haired "Garfield" type, who didn't miss too many meals. Bear was an enormous cat, hence the name. But though he was absolutely ferocious-looking, he was a real wimp.

The nice folks we bought our home from had at least six cats. When they moved out they could only take a few with them; so they left two behind, hoping they would go next door to their father's place. But cats are very territorial by nature. The two left

69

behind were a small male and a pretty little female. As far as they were concerned this was still home.

Well, on the Monday morning I left for South America, Carla let Bear out to explore his new domain. The male cat left behind, feeling threatened by this new kid on the block, commenced to whip the fire out of 'ol Bear, and so off he ran. To this day we haven't found him, but the other cat is still hanging around. Poor dumb 'ol Bear! No telling where he is or what kind of living conditions he is experiencing, if indeed he is still alive.

Think of it! I am the new landlord and the property is legally mine. This means my cats have a right to be on that piece of land. The other cats are aliens. I would have backed Bear up. Plus, Bear was twice the size of the other male and probably twice as strong but he was a big, spoiled, pampered baby. Like a lot of Christians, he looked good but had no fight in him. What a great lesson for all of us. Jesus is our Lord. He has created and owns every square foot of planet earth.

The earth is the Lord's and all its fullness, the world and those who dwell therein (Ps. 24:1).

Satan is the god of this world, or system (Cosmos), but the earth belongs to God and God's people. We have been given power and authority to take back what the devil usurped. But the principalities believe they have rights too. Just like the male cat who marked out his boundaries, the wicked spirits over our cities have staked out their claim as overlords. They will not go away simply because you and I are professing Christians. The two cats didn't leave simply because we moved in. They'll have to be either forced to leave or submit to my authority. We can learn a great deal about the demon world by studying the animal kingdom. Many things animals do are by program.

As I mentioned in *Storming Hell's Brazen Gates*, there is no love or camaraderie between evil spirits. They do what Satan tells them because he is their lord. The only feelings they have are fear, hate, jealousy, anger, pride, confusion and the like. Worship, praise and intercession always send a shock wave through their camp and temporarily cause great confusion. That is why people are more open to the gospel message after praise and worship, good teaching and prayer. The evil spirits harassing them with lies are for a short time bound, and their minds are clear to make a decision for Christ.

Ministers at every service must act quickly to seize the moment while the kingdom of darkness is in disarray because of the great light and power coming down through the proclamation of truth and the prayer of the believers. I give five invitations every time I minister; salvation, rededication, baptism of the Holy Ghost, deliverance from demons and healing for the body. I figure, while the anointing has our enemies on the run, go for it all!

My dear friend and neighbor, Dr. C.M. Ward wrote:

I am on a planet where Satan is boss (of the system), and he doesn't like me. My testimony is a menace to his administration. He will mislead me if possible. He applies pressure. He adapts to my age, my experience, and to my circumstances. I live under the stimulus of constant invitation. The devil... showeth him (Mt..4:8). The lure is there. Suggestion is heavy. (C.M. Ward, Revivaltime Pulpit, No. 23, p. 38)

These comments by Dr. Ward are all too true, but God's plan of redemption and take-over is hell's frustration: "for we are not ignorant of his (Satan's) devices" (2 Cor. 2:11). "Put on the whole armor of God, that you may be able to stand against the wiles of the devil" (Eph. 6:11). Knowing our enemy and discerning his boundaries and limitations is essential.

Satan himself marks out certain areas to situate his seat of government. In the book of Ezekiel we see him over an ancient place called Tyre.

Moreover the word of the Lord came to me, saying, "Son of man, take up a lamentation for the king of Tyre, and say to him, 'Thus says the Lord God: "You were the seal of perfection, full of wisdom and perfect in beauty. You were in Eden,

71

the garden of God; every precious stone was your covering: The sardius, topaz, and diamond, beryl, onyx, and jasper, sapphire, turquoise, and emerald with gold. The workmanship of your timbrels and pipes was prepared for you on the day you were created. You were the anointed cherub who covers; I established you; You were on the holy mountain of God; you walked back and forth in the midst of fiery stones. You were perfect in your ways from the day you were created, till iniquity was found in you. By the abundance of your trading you became filled with violence within, and you sinned; therefore I cast you as a profane thing out of the mountain of God; and I destroyed you, O covering cherub, from the midst of the fiery stones. Your heart was lifted up because of your beauty; you corrupted your wisdom for the sake of your splendor; I cast you to the ground, I laid you before kings, that they might gaze at you. You defiled your sanctuaries by the multitude of your iniquities, by the iniquity of your trading; therefore I brought fire from your midst; it devoured you, and I turned you to ashes upon the earth in the sight of all who saw you. All who knew you among the peoples are astonished at you; you have become a horror, and shall be no more forever" ' " (Ezek. 28:11-19).

Satanic governments always parallel human governments. Notice as we read the first part of Ezekiel 28 that there is a literal kingdom of Tyre.

The word of the Lord came to me again, saying, "Son of man, say to the prince of Tyre, 'Thus says the Lord God: "Because your heart is lifted up, and you say, I am a god, I sit in the seat of gods, in the midst of the seas, yet you are a man, and not a god, as the heart of a god (Behold, you are wiser than Daniel! There is no secret that can be hidden from you! With your wisdom and your understanding you have gained riches for yourself, and gathered gold and silver into your treasuries; by your great wisdom in trade you have increased your riches, and your heart is lifted up because of your riches), " therefore thus says the Lord God: "Because you have

*set your heart as the heart of a god, behold, therefore, I will
bring strangers against you, the most terrible of the nations;
and they shall draw their swords against the beauty of your
wisdom, and defile your splendor, they shall throw you down
into the Pit, and you shall die the death of the slain in the
midst of the seas. Will you still say before him who slays you, I
am a god? But you shall be a man, and not a god, in the hand
of him who slays you. You shall die the death of the uncir-
cumcised by the hand of aliens; for I have spoken," says the
Lord God'* "* (Ezek. 28:1-10).

Notice, "prince of Tyre" and "you are a man, and not a god,"
in verse 2. Yet, we see Satan referred to as, "the king of Tyre" in
verse 11. Also note in verse 14, "you were the anointed cherub
(angel) who covers (had power and authority)." Verse 12 makes
reference to him being in the garden of Eden. Centuries later we
find our adversary has moved his seat to a city in Asia Minor
called Pergamos.

*And to the angel of the church in Pergamos write, "These
things says He who has the sharp two-edged sword: 'I know
your works, and where you dwell, where Satan's throne is.
And you hold fast to my name, and did not deny My faith
even in the days in which Antipas was My faithful martyr,
who was killed among you, where Satan dwells' "* (Rev.
2:12-13).

Pergamos was called "the Cathedral City." It was given over
to idolatry. The city was also a place of great political influence,
and many laws were passed condemning this new dangerous
movement called Christianity. Satan's seat or throne is no longer
over Pergamos but you'll find him in a modern version of it.

In studying cities, we find a startling similarity from nation to
nation. Port cities all seem to have the same problems — San
Francisco, Los Angeles, New York, Rio de Janeiro, Hong Kong,
cities all along the Mediterranean, and the list continues. In these
ports of entry or gateway cities we find spirits of lust, revelry,
greed, lawlessness, witchcraft and so on. Yet the more you move

inland you come up against religious spirits or spirits of tradition. I've seen this in several countries I've visited. An African evangelist from Nigeria referred to the coastal principalities as "water spirits." It is not really clear to us but it is obvious that some spirits are attracted to water. The cities around the sea of Galilee were infested with demoniacs who were the wild type. An interesting scripture to look at is Matthew 12:43:

When an unclean spirit goes out of a man, he goes through DRY places, seeking rest and finds none.

These "dry places" bring confusion, unrest, even torment to these unclean spirits. The Indians of the American plains used water when dealing with certain spirits, especially the spirit of death.

Getting back to looking at cities, yours and mine, have you ever noticed how each one has its own unique personality? The reason is simple. Every prince, ruler or dark power has his own personality. A community will conform to it if he's not broken and removed. The good news is that Satan and his kind are limited. Through Christ, you and I are not!

You have made him to have dominion over the works of Your hands; You have put all things under his feet... (Ps. 8:6).

The ancient pagans understood territorial lordship

Then the servants of the king of Syria said to him, "Their gods are gods of the hills. Therefore they were stronger than we; but if we fight against them in the plain, then surely we will be stronger than they" (1 Kings 20:23).

But, the God we serve is not limited to a particular territory or to a certain kind of terrain.

Then a man of God came and spoke to the king of Israel, and said, "Thus says the Lord: Because the Syrians have said, 'The Lord is God of the hills, but He is not God of the valleys,' therefore I will deliver all this great multitude into your hand, and you shall know that I am the Lord" (1 Kings 20:28).

Of course, the most graphic picture of territorial principalities is found in Daniel 10:12-13:

> *Then he said to me, "Do not fear, Daniel, for from the first day that you set your heart to understand, and to humble yourself before your God, your words were heard; and I have come because of your words. But the prince of the kingdom of Persia withstood me twenty-one days; and behold, Michael, one of the chief princes, came to help me, for I had been left alone there with the kings of Persia."*

Apparently, the perimeters of the ancient Persian empire were boundaries of the ruling prince and his subordinates. A parallel kingdom of government in the "heavenlies" was set up exactly over man-made boundaries. The messenger angel sent to Daniel went on to say,

> *Then again, the one having the likeness of a man touched me and strengthened me. And he said, "O man greatly beloved, fear not! Peace be to you; be strong, yes, be strong!" So when he spoke to me I was strengthened, and said, "Let my lord speak, for you have strengthened me." Then he said, "Do you know why I have come to you? And now I must return to fight with the prince of Persia; and when I have gone forth, indeed the prince of Greece will come"* (Dan. 10:18-20).

Notice, the prince of Greece is mentioned. One only has to be reminded of recent events in modern Persia (Iran-Iraq) to be aware of the power of the prince. All the problems that part of the world, including the Persian Gulf, has caused — the horrible conflict between Iran-Iraq, the foiled attempt to rescue American hostages during the Carter administration, etc., are a constant warning to people of discernment of what could happen here if we don't pull down the prince over America and the ruling spirits over our cities.

While I was in Argentina, I interviewed several leading pastors. A beautiful brother by the name of Norberto Carlini, who pastors a thriving work in the city of Rosario, told me a fascinating story of his humble beginnings. This city was given over to spiritists and witchcraft. The traditional Catholic church was there, but there was no real move of God to speak of. Great resistance was felt by evangelists who tried to break through the stronghold.

At Pastor Carlini's inaugural service, many demon-possessed people were present, and a spirit gripped him to the point of near suffocation. The people began to threaten him and warn him to go away. "You're not wanted here, go!" they yelled. The flabbergasted minister whispered the name above every name. "Please, Jesus, help me!" was his cry. The evil presence lifted, and the stubborn man of God was not intimidated but dug in and fought for the city.

Early in his work there he had a remarkable experience. The custom in Argentina, as well as in many Latin countries, is to go to the priest for help, and if he can't lend assistance then to go to the spiritists. One recent convert of Carlini's had been separated from his wife and wanted her back. He, like many, had gone to a woman spiritist to plead his case. The woman promised to put a spell on his wife and force her back. The new pastor in town asked if he could accompany him, incognito of course.

As the pastor sat and listened to this witch tell his new member what she intended to do, he couldn't take it any longer. "Senora," he piped up, "how can you help my friend when you yourself are all bound up?"

"Why don't you go back to your little church, preacher," the angry woman retorted.

"How do you know I am a preacher?" asked Carlini.

"A voice told me," she replied.

"Answer me this if you will," the bold minister pressed on. "Why can't you sleep on Tuesdays and Fridays?"

The woman's eyes widened with unbelief. "Who told you that?" she insisted. "How do you know this?"

Carlini knew this because most witchcraft and occultic practices are done on those two days. The demon world becomes excited because of all the activity. Spells, charms, curses and so on, are believed by the practitioners to have much more power on those days. Because of it the evil spirits in this poor woman were activated more than usual and she couldn't find rest.

These misguided souls believe they get their powers from God. Pastor Carlini eventually delivered this woman from her tormentors, and she is now a member of his church. She later told him her powers were limited by two rivers several miles apart. She could only work her magic within the confines of those two boundaries. Sounds a little like the story of Simon the sorcerer.

But there was a certain man called Simon, who previously practiced sorcery in the city and astonished the people of Samaria, claiming that he was someone great, to whom they all gave heed, from the least to the greatest, saying, "This man is the great power of God." And they heeded him because he had astonished them with his sorceries for a long time. But when they believed Philip as he preached the things concerning the Kingdom of God and the name of Jesus Christ, both men and women were baptized (Acts 8:9-12).

Simon's powers were limited to Samaria!

As I mentioned before, my close friend, Ed Silvoso, an Argentine minister who spends his time shuttling between his homeland and San Jose, California, where his American base is, told me a most fascinating story. A pastor had a run-in with a demonized individual who seemed to be controlling a wide area. The preacher had several conflicts with this stubborn, arrogant spirit.

A short time after Argentina had beat West Germany in the final game of the World Cup soccer playoffs, the preacher asked the evil entity what he thought of the match. What led the man of God to do this escapes me but the answer was shocking. With a deep, thick German accent, the demon said, "Terrible, we should have won." The startled pastor asked, "We, you sound like a German patriot."

The spirit speaking through its female host with a man's voice went on to brag about his exploits and assignments while stationed in West Germany. The prince of the power of the air had since reassigned him to this region in Argentina. With revival ready to break out in many places in South America, it is little wonder that Satan would ship fresh, strong troops to try and thwart the move of God. The preacher pressed in with Scripture, reminding his evil enemy that his Commander in Chief, Jesus Christ, beat his commander in chief, Satan, and because of that truth must obey him and leave the area.

The next encounter was almost amusing. The spirit was whimpering like a spanked pup. "What's wrong with you?" asked the pastor. "I've been replaced by one stronger," replied the beaten foe. Soon after this final meeting the woman moved away. A stronger one never came. Don't ever trust the testimony of a demon. He was soundly whipped by a child of God and he knew it. Demons only tell the truth if it is convenient or if they are more afraid of you than they are of their master.

When Jesus confronted the wild man among the tombs and demanded, "What is your name?" the petrified demon leader responded, "My name is Legion; for we are many," and begged earnestly that he not be sent out of the country" (Mk. 5:9-10). Two significant points of interest. They told Jesus the truth out of fear, and they begged Him not to send them out of their territory or assigned country. Demons have a tremendous fear of Jesus.

Then they came to the other side of the sea, to the country of the Gadarenes. And when He had come out of the boat, immediately there met Him out of the tombs a man with an unclean spirit, who had his dwelling among the tombs; and no one could bind him, not even with chains, because he had often been bound with shackles and chains. And the chains had been pulled apart by him, and the shackles broken in pieces; neither could anyone tame him. And always, night and day, he was in the mountains and in the tombs, crying out and cutting himself with stones. But when he saw Jesus from afar, he ran and worshiped Him. And he cried out with a loud voice and said, "What have I to do with You, Jesus, Son of the Most High God? I implore You by God that You do not torment me" (Mk. 5:1-7).

Earlier in His ministry, we read of another demon encounter:

Then they went into Capernaum, and immediately on the Sabbath He entered the synagogue and taught. And they were astonished at His teaching, for He taught them as one having authority, and not as the scribes. Now there was a man in their synagogue with an unclean spirit. And he cried out, saying, "Let us alone! What have we to do with You, Jesus of Nazareth? Did You come to destroy us? I know who You are — the Holy One of God!" But Jesus rebuked him, saying, "Be quiet and come out of him!" And when the unclean spirit had convulsed him and cried out with a loud voice, he came out of him. Then they were all amazed, so that they questioned among themselves saying, "What is this? What new doctrine is this? For with authority He commands even the unclean spirits, and they obey Him" (Mk. 1:21-27).

Can this fear and respect be transferred to the believer? Once again, we read in Matthew 28:18-19,

Then Jesus came and spoke to them, saying, "All authority has been given Me in heaven and on earth. Go therefore..."

Christ commissioned His disciples to go forth confidently, knowing they were backed by His authority. In effect, He was saying, "I have deputized you to carry on My mission. You have My seal of approval and authority to carry on what I started." Paul confirms that our "spiritual arsenal" is more than adequate to wage warfare victoriously.

For though we walk in the flesh, we do not war according to the flesh. For the weapons of our warfare are not carnal but mighty in God for pulling down strongholds (2 Cor. 10:3-4).

May the hordes of Hell tremble at our presence!

CHAPTER 12

The Power of Faith

And Peter, remembering, said to Him, "Rabbi, look! The fig tree which You cursed has withered away." So Jesus answered and said to them, "Have faith in God. For assuredly, I say to you, whoever says to this mountain, Be removed and be cast into the sea, and does not doubt in his heart, but believes that those things he says will come to pass, he will have whatever he says" (Mk. 11:21-23).

In the seventies a heavy emphasis was placed on the subject of faith. Scripture slogans like, "I believe I receive" or "Keep standing on the Word" became fairly widespread and popular. Making the proper confession was essential if you were a real "Word person." Please don't get me wrong; these were, and still are, valid beliefs even though some have gone beyond the Bible under the banner of "faith."

In Mark 11, we have the classic teaching and example by Jesus of how faith can work. The chapter begins with His glorious entrance into Jerusalem, the crowds cheering wildly.

Then they brought the colt to Jesus and threw their garments on it, and He sat on it. And many spread their garments on the road, and others cut down leafy branches from the trees and spread them on the road. Then those who went before and those who followed cried out, saying: "Hosanna! Blessed is He who comes in the name of the Lord! Blessed is the kingdom of our father David that comes in the name of the Lord! Hosanna in the highest!" And Jesus went into Jerusalem and into the temple. So when He had looked

*around at all things, as the hour was already late, He went
out to Bethany with the twelve* (Mk. 11:7-11).

After looking "around at all things" that were going on in the
temple, Jesus apparently lost His appetite for food and fasted
until morning. No doubt He was praying to the Father, seeking
wisdom and direction for the next day's visit to the temple.

Faith to Curse and Remove

*Now the next day, when they had come out from Bethany,
he was hungry. And seeing from afar a fig tree having leaves,
He went to see if perhaps He would find something on it. And
when He came to it, He found nothing but leaves, for it was
not the season for figs. In response Jesus said to it, "Let no one
eat fruit from you ever again." And His disciples heard it*
(Mk. 11:12-14).

The fruitless fig tree no doubt reminded Him of the nation of
Israel: great promise but no performance! He was at first expec-
tant and then soon disappointed. From a distance the tree looked
good, leafy and apparently full of figs, but a close scrutiny
produced not one single fruit. We read Jotham's parable in
Judges 9:10-11,

*Then the trees said to the fig tree, "You come and reign
over us!" But the fig tree said to them, "Should I cease my
sweetness and my good fruit, and go to sway over trees?"*

Commenting on Jotham's parable, Matthew Henry writes:

*Sweetness and good fruit are, in Jotham's parable, the
honour of the fig tree, and its serviceableness therein to man,
preferable to the preferment of being promoted over the trees;
now to be deprived of that was a grievous curse. This was
intended to be a type and figure of the doom passed upon the
Jewish church, to which he came, seeking fruit, but found
none* (Matthew Henry's Commentary, Book of Mark, Mac-
Donald Publishing, p. 527).

With the same authority He used to curse the fig tree Jesus
cleanses the temple as a Son in His own house. Notice no one
attempted to stop Him. When the spirit of purging and righteous
judgment comes, even the most cynical know right from wrong.

So they came to Jerusalem. And Jesus went into the temple and began to drive out those who bought and sold in the temple, and overturned the tables of the moneychangers and the seats of those who sold doves. And He would not allow anyone to carry wares through the temple. Then He taught, saying to them, "Is it not written, My house shall be called a house of prayer for all nations? But you have made it a den of thieves." And the scribes and chief priests heard it and sought how they might destroy Him; for they feared Him, because all the people were astonished at His teaching (Mk. 11:15-18).

Faith has Permanent Results

Now in the morning, as they passed by, they saw the fig tree dried up from the roots. And Peter, remembering, said to Him, "Rabbi, look! The fig tree which You cursed has withered away." So Jesus answered and said to them, "Have faith in God" (Mk. 11:20-22).

The curse Jesus placed on the fig tree was not seasonal, but permanent. The leaves would never cheat another hungry soul! The only use this tree would have would be for fuel, not for food.

The withered tree seemed to surprise Peter, as well as the other disciples. "Rabbi, look!" (Mk. 11:21). The disciples admired the power of command which Jesus manifested and longed to exercise similar authority.

Jesus said they could if they, "Have faith in God" (Mk. 11:22) or, literally, "Have the faith of God!"

Now notice His divine instructions carefully. "For assuredly, I say to you, whoever says to this mountain, 'Be removed...' " (Mk. 11:23).

We've been taught that faith is something we use to receive the blessings of God. Here, in Mark 11, the emphasis of our Lord's teaching is first to curse unfruitfulness and remove obstacles and obstructions; then we are in a position to "believe that we receive."

A postscript is added in verses 25-26:

And whenever you stand praying, if you have anything against anyone, forgive him, that your Father in heaven may also forgive you your trespasses. But if you do not forgive neither will your Father in heaven forgive your trespasses.

Unforgiveness, bitterness, wrath and such must be constantly cursed and removed if our prayers are to be answered. The point I am endeavoring to make is this: We all want revival in our cities and churches. We pray for it, beg God for it, preach about it; but we will never experience it unless we first curse and remove principalities and powers and open the brazen skies above our cities. Then the blessings of God will fall in a mighty way. I suggest strongly that you read again pages two and three of my book, *Storming Hell's Brazen Gates*. We must certainly remember the sobering truth of Ephesians 6:12,

For we do not wrestle against flesh and blood, but against principalities, against powers, against the rulers of the darkness of this age, against spiritual wickedness in the heavenly places.

I was recently holding a warfare conference in Kileen, Texas, for my friend, Pastor Terry Whitley, and his wife Jan. We were all sitting around his office between services discussing Eph. 6:12. Jan said she had recently read in a commentary that in ancient times the wrestling matches were far more serious and final than in the Hollywood versions we see today. The penalty for losing was having your eyes put out. Think of it! If you lost, you never saw again. If we lose our "holy war" against the forces of evil, will we ever see the harvest, the awakening, the move of God's Spirit we crave to see?

We must learn to exercise "the faith of God." We must not be afraid to command and remove unwanted entities from our cities. Remember, we have a Captain to fight for, a banner to fight under, a cause greater than our own, and certain rules of war by which to be governed. In this regard I quote Matthew Henry:

The combat for which we are to be prepared is not against ordinary human enemies, not barely against men compounded of flesh and blood, nor against our own corrupt natures singly considered, but against the several ranks of devils, who

have a government which they exercise in this world. (1) We have to do with a subtle enemy, an enemy who uses wiles and stratagems, as vs. 11. He has a thousand ways of beguiling unstable souls: hence he is called a serpent for subtlety, an old serpent, experienced in the art and trade of tempting. (2) He is a powerful enemy: Principalities, and powers, and rulers. They are numerous, they are vigorous; and rule in those heathen nations which are yet in darkness. The dark parts of the world are the seat of Satan's empire. Yea, they are usurping princes over all men who are yet in a state of sin and ignorance. Satan's is a kingdom of darkness; whereas Christ's is a kingdom of light. (Matthew Henry's Commentary, The Ephesians, MacDonald Publishing, p. 719)

It is interesting to me that Satan is referred to as a reptile (i.e. serpent, dragon). Subtlety was and is a natural characteristic of serpents, along with cunning and craftiness. No wonder Satan picked this creature to possess and speak through.

A minister friend shared with me an article he read on the "reptilian mind," and I'd like to share parts of it with you.

Reptilian Mind

A term more readily used by the medical community is "the limbic nervous system." Let me give you a definition from the Dorland's Illustrated Medical Dictionary, 26th Edition (1981), and then perhaps you can see why some call this the "reptilian mind."

Limbic system: a term closely applied to a group of brain structures common to all mammals associated with olfaction but of greater importance in other activities, such as automatic functions and certain aspects of emotion and behavior.

This interesting name, "the reptilian mind" or the limbic nervous system, opens more than a few avenues of thought on how Satan (the serpent, dragon) influences the behavior and emotions of hyper-religious people.

The most subtle, yet dangerous evil spirit is the "religious" spirit. A religious spirit keeps people in bondage to rituals and traditions (man-made doctrines) and blinds them to truth. Satan understands man's basic need to worship a higher power, so he invents a diversity of beliefs. The Bible makes reference to "doctrines of devils" (1 Tim. 4:1).

It is obvious in observing religious people that they are not "possessed" in the classic sense of the word, with bulging eyes and foaming mouths screaming obscenities, but they are obsessed with their beliefs. In most cases there are distinct patterns or rituals associated with their particular religion, especially when there is a frenzied or fevered pitch.

I've been around the world and preached on several continents. Recently I watched a celebration at the Wailing Wall in Jerusalem. As I observed the men jerking and bowing in front of their shrine, I had such compassion for them. How many times have we witnessed Hare Krishnas going through their gyrations or seen on television Moslems doing strange ceremonial rites from some middle-eastern country.

As a young boy looking for adventure, I was always excited to find a lizard sunning itself on a rock. I would sit mesmerized by its bobbing and weaving motions. Reptiles are some of the most ritualistic of all animals. These cold-blooded vertebrates have dances and rhythmic moves that send out various signals. It is striking how religious zealots appear "reptilian-like" when expressing devotion to their object of devotion. Could it be this part of the human mind is what Satan goes after? We see Catholics who know very little about the Bible, yet they cross themselves, count beads, and do an assortment of other religious things in place of knowledge.

Faith Tears Down Strongholds!

God demands that the "high places" of idol worship be totally torn down. Courageous faith accepts the challenge!

Even today the cults of "high places" still exist, under a modified form. If you've ever travelled the Middle East you may remember seeing Mukams which crown almost every hill. Like the Chinese worship of the dead, the Fellahin openly worship at these shrines. The small whitewashed domes (Kubbeh) or stations are sacred "high places" to the peasants.

On a trip to India, I was surprised to see so many small one-man Hindu shrines dotting the countryside, especially the mountains or hilltops. The higher the worshippers can get, geographically speaking, the closer they feel they are to their gods.

Similarly, the Canaanites had their Mukams or shrines dedicated to the worship of Baal, Ashtoreth, Chemosh, Molech, Milcom and other lesser-known gods. Every now and then in the chronicle of the Kings we find a reformer who understood the way to bring revival.

> So Abijah rested with his fathers, and they buried him in the City of David. Then Asa his son reigned in his place. In his days the land was quiet for ten years.
>
> Asa did what was good and right in the eyes of the Lord his God, for he removed the altars of the foreign gods and the high places, and broke down the sacred pillars and cut down the wooden images. He commanded Judah to seek the Lord God of their fathers, and to observe the law and the commandment. He also removed the high places and the incense altars from all the cities of Judah, and the kingdom was quiet under him. And he built fortified cities in Judah, for the land had rest; he had no war in those years, because the Lord had given him rest. Therefore he said to Judah, "Let us build these cities and make walls around them, and towers, gates, and bars, while the land is yet before us because we have sought the Lord our God; we have sought Him, and He has given us rest on every side." So they built and prospered (2 Chron. 14:1-7).

One of my favorite stories in the Old Testament is found in 2 Kings 22-23. Young king Josiah is surrounded by demon worship, the New Age (Babylonian religions), sodomy, the killing of babies, and astrology. Sounds like modern America, doesn't it?

Josiah puts up with all this for awhile. Like most bleeding-heart ultra-liberals of today who have a 'live and let live' attitude,

Josiah thought, "Hey, if people want to do weird things that's their business. It's not hurting anyone, especially me and my family. Let people do their thing."

But one day early in his reign he received the shock of his young life. The Word of God had been hidden for years. Josiah had never seen an early version of the law, but in the process of cleaning out and repairing the temple a musty old copy was found. The story reads,

> Then Hilkiah the high priest said to Shaphan the scribe, "I have found the Book of the Law in the house of the Lord." And Hilkiah gave the book to Shaphan, and he read it. So Shaphan the scribe went to the king, bringing the king word, saying, "Your servants have gathered the money that was found in the house, and have delivered it into the hand of those who do the work, who oversee the house of the Lord." Then Shaphan the scribe showed the king, saying, "Hilkiah the priest has given me a book." And Shaphan read it before the king. Now it happened, when the king heard the words of the Book of the Law, then he tore his clothes. Then the king commanded Hilkiah the priest, Ahikam the son of Shaphan, Achbor, the son of Michaiah, Shaphan the scribe, and Asaiah a servant of the king, saying, "Go, inquire of the Lord for me, for the people and for all Judah, concerning the words of this book that has been found; for great is the wrath of the Lord that is aroused against us, because our fathers have not obeyed the words of this book, to do according to all that is written concerning us" (2 Kings 22:8-13).

"My God!" he must have exclaimed as the Word of the Lord filled his ears and heart for the first time. "We are headed for utter destruction if something isn't done quickly!" So being king, he moved with authority, and being Hebrew and a covenant child, with conviction. Here's the amazing account of what followed:

> And the king commanded Hilkiah the high priest, the priests of the second order, and the doorkeepers, to bring out of the temple of the Lord all the articles that were made for

Baal, for Asherah, and for all the host of heaven, and he burned them outside Jerusalem in the fields of Kidron, and carried their ashes to Bethel. Then he removed the idolatrous priests whom the kings of Judah had ordained to burn incense on the high places in the cities of Judah and in the places all around Jerusalem, and those who burned incense to Baal, to the sun, to the moon, to the constellations, and to all the host of heaven. And he brought out the wooden image from the house of the Lord, to the Brook Kidron outside Jerusalem, burned it at the Brook Kidron and ground it to ashes, and threw its ashes on the graves of the common people. Then he tore down the ritual booths of the perverted persons that were in the house of the Lord, where the women wove hangings for the wooden image. And he brought all the priests from the cities of Judah, and defiled the high places where the priests had burned incense, from Geba to Beersheba; also he broke down the high places at the gates which were at the entrance of the Gate of Joshua the governor of the city, which were to the left of the city gate. Nevertheless the priests of the high places did not come up to the altar of the Lord in Jerusalem, but they ate unleavened bread among their brethren. And he defiled Topheth, which is in the Valley of the Son of Hinnom, that no man might make his son or his daughter pass through the fire of Molech. Then he removed the horses that the kings of Judah had dedicated to the sun, at the entrance to the house of the Lord, by the chamber of Nathan-Melech, the officer who was in the court; and he burned the chariots of the sun with fire. The altars that were on the roof, the upper chamber of Ahaz, which the kings of Judah had made, and the altars which Manasseh had made in the two courts of the house of the Lord, the king broke down and pulverized there, and threw their dust into the Brook Kidron. Then the king defiled the high places that were east of Jerusalem, which were on the south of the Mount of Corruption, which Solomon king of Israel had built for Ashtoreth the abomination of the Sidonians, for Chemosh the abomination of the Moabites, and for Milcom the abomination of the people of Ammon. And he broke in pieces the sacred pillars and cut down the wooden images, and filled their places with the bones of men.

Moreover, the altar that was at Bethel and the high place which Jeroboam the son of Nebat, who made Israel sin, had made, both that altar and the high place he broke down; and he burned the high place and crushed it to powder, and he burned the wooden image. As Josiah turned, he saw the tombs that were on the mountain. And he sent and took the bones out of the tombs and burned them on the altar, and defiled it according to the word of the Lord which the men of God proclaimed, who proclaimed these words. Then he said, "What gravestone is this that I see?" And the men of the city told him, "It is the tomb of the man of God who came from Judah and proclaimed these things which you have done against the altar of Bethel." And he said, "Let him alone; let no one move his bones." So they let his bones alone, with the bones of the prophet who came from Samaria. Then Josiah also took away all the shrines of the high places that were in the cities of Samaria, which the kings of Israel had made to provoke the Lord to anger; and he did to them according to all the deeds he had done in Bethel. He executed all the priests of the high places who were there on the altars, and burned men's bones on them; and he returned to Jerusalem.

Then the king commanded all the people, saying, "Keep the Passover to the Lord your God, as it is written in this Book of the Covenant." Surely such a Passover had never been held since the days of the judges who judged Israel, nor in all the days of the kings of Israel and the kings of Judah. But in the eighteenth year of King Josiah this Passover was held before the Lord in Jerusalem. Moreover Josiah put away those who consulted mediums and spiritists, the household gods and idols, all the abominations that were seen in the land of Judah and in Jerusalem, that he might perform the words of the law which were written in the book that Hilkiah the priest found in the house of the Lord. Now before him there was no king like him, who turned to the Lord with all his heart, with all his soul, and with all his might, according to all the Law of Moses; nor after him did any arise like him (2 Kings 23:4-25).

Are you getting the picture yet? There are many who are doing good and preaching truth, but the "high places" have not been removed. Again, I remind you,

> *For we wrestle not against flesh and blood, but against principalities, against powers, against the rulers of the darkness of this world, against spiritual wickedness in high places* (Eph. 6:12, KJV).

From these high places come strongholds against righteousness. But again the Word of God assures us,

> *For though we walk in the flesh, we do not war according to the flesh. For the weapons of our warfare are not carnal but mighty in God for pulling down strongholds, casting down arguments and every high thing that exalts itself against the knowledge of God, bringing every thought into captivity to the obedience of Christ* (2 Cor. 10:3-5).

For every weapon our enemy has, we have one better! And, best of all, we have a greater Commander in Chief dwelling within.

> *For You are of God, little children, and have overcome them, because He who is in you is greater than he who is in the world* (1 Jn. 4:4).

Man's wars and the Church's war have many common denominators. Just the other night I was watching one of those cable networks that features documentaries. That particular night the focus was on General Dwight D. Eisenhower and the allied invasion of Normandy. The preparation and the behind-the-scenes planning took far more time than the actual assault and ensuing victory. Even though the American Commander in Chief and his British counterparts didn't always see eye to eye, the cause far outweighed ego and protocol. Evangelicals and Charismatics better learn this lesson quickly.

Many wanted to march straight on to Berlin, estimating no more than 100,000 would lose their lives in taking that key city. Ike said, "No, we will methodically cut off Berlin's supplies and the city will surrender." History proves General Eisenhower was right. Not one man on our side lost his life as the allies marched in to a defeated city. Many good men paid a stiff price in getting there, but the final outcome was total victory!

Hebrews, chapter 11, tells us of the great men and women of faith who paid a great price to bring the church this far. Dare we let them down?

CHAPTER 13

Idolatry — The Spirit of Confusion

And God spoke all these words, saying: "I am the Lord your God, who brought you out of the land of Egypt, out of the house of bondage. You shall have no other gods before Me. You shall not make for yourself any carved image, or any likeness of anything that is in heaven above, or that is in the earth beneath, or that is in the water under the earth; you shall not bow down to them nor serve them. For I, the Lord your God, am a jealous God, visiting the iniquity of the fathers on the children to the third and fourth generations of those who hate Me, but showing mercy to thousands, to those who love Me and keep My commandments" (Ex. 20:1-6).

Even though I touched on this subject in chapter 1, I feel a need to press on a bit concerning this vital truth.

In Isaiah's prophecy against idolatrous cities we read, "The city of confusion is broken down; every house is shut up, so that none may go in" (Is. 24:10).

The theme of Isaiah 41 is the futility of false gods or idols, as the following verses illustrate:

"Present your case," says the Lord. "Bring forth your strong reasons," says the King of Jacob. "Let them bring forth and show us what will happen; Let them show the former things, what they were, That we may consider them, and know the latter end of them; or declare to us things to come. Show the things that are to come hereafter, that we may know that you are gods; Yes, do good or do evil, that we may be

dismayed and see it together. Indeed you are nothing. And your work is nothing; He who chooses you is an abomination" (Is. 41:21-24).

Indeed they are all worthless; their works are nothing; Their molded images are wind and confusion (Is. 41:29)

We read further in Isaiah 45:14-17:

Thus says the Lord: "The labor of Egypt and merchandise of Cush and the Sabeans, men of stature, shall come over to you, and they shall be yours; they shall walk behind you, they shall come over the chains; and they shall bow down to you. They will make supplication to you, saying, 'Surely God is in you, and there is no other; there is no other God.' " Truly You are God, who hide Yourself, O God of Israel, the Savior! They shall be ashamed and also disgraced, all of them; They shall go in confusion together, who are makers of idols. But Israel shall be saved by the Lord with an everlasting salvation; You shall not be ashamed or disgraced forever and ever (Is. 45:14-17).

In the New Testament when Paul came to the ultra-idolatrous city of Ephesus, where the worship of Diana was prominent, he began to preach and persuade and "turned away many people, saying that they are not gods which are made with hands" (Acts 19:26).

The passage goes on to say in verse 29: "So the whole city was filled with confusion..."

Confusion is one of Satan's chief weapons of warfare. People who can't think right rarely make good decisions. Look at third-world countries where idolatry is practiced; you'll see confused governments, confused monetary systems, confused traffic, confused everything!

Our American idols may not be carved out of gold, silver, wood or stone. They may not come in the image of a creature or of a demon-inspired, hideous-looking gargoyle, but we do have them. An idol can also be an object or person who has our love, time and admiration, anything that keeps a person away from

God, His church and the saints. Our careers, hobbies, family, house, television, sports, boyfriends, girlfriends, etc., can be classified as such if they have our hearts. Should we then be surprised to read in our leading national magazines that a third of America's populace is depressed and confused.

For they themselves declare concerning us what manner of entry we had to you, and how you turned to God from idols to serve the living and true God (1 Thess. 1:9).

Confusion brings spiritual blindness. We are commissioned to open the eyes of the blind with the truth of God's Word.

whose minds the god of this age has blinded, who do not believe, lest the light of the gospel of the glory of Christ, who is the image of God, should shine on them. For we do not preach ourselves, but Christ Jesus the Lord, and ourselves your servants for Jesus' sake. For it is the God who commanded light to shine out of darkness who has shone in our hearts to give the light of the knowledge of the glory of God in the face of Jesus Christ (2 Cor. 4:4-6).

With authority we command the strong man of confusion to desist, while with compassion we untie the blindfolds from the floundering masses.

and to make all people see what is the fellowship of the mystery, which from the beginning of the ages has been hidden in God who created all things through Jesus Christ, to the intent that now the manifold wisdom of God might be made known by the church to the principalities and powers in the heavenly places, according to the eternal purpose which He accomplished in Christ Jesus our Lord (Eph. 3:9-11).

CHAPTER 14

Another Look At
Binding and Loosing

*And I will give you the keys to the kingdom of heaven, and
whatever you bind on earth will be bound in heaven, and
whatever you loose on earth will be loosed in heaven* (Mt.
16:19).

The metaphor here is that of a castle or house with locked
gates and the only way to get in is to use the proper keys. The one
with the keys is like a steward.

Isaiah carries this theme in chapter 22, verse 22:

*The key of the house of David I will lay on his shoulder; So
he shall open, and no one shall shut; and he shall shut, and no
one shall open.*

In modern times when one is given the keys to a city it symbolizes
the handing over of authority. Peter, and later the other disciples,
are promised a certain authority. Part of that authority is the
power to bind and loose. Binding and loosing has been taught
from several different viewpoints. The English words 'bind' and
'loose' may have been a poor choice for the translators to pick,
but nevertheless they did. A better rendering is to 'forbid' or
'allow.' To bind is to forbid, to pronounce unlawful; to loose is to
allow or declare lawful. These expressions were found in the
Talmud and to the Hebrew mind were quite understandable.
The Pharisees had the power to determine what was lawful or
unlawful. For instance, the Word of the Lord commanded the
Sabbath as a day of rest — no work! But wait, what is described

as work and what isn't? The priests had to make judgments and their say was final.

In the kingdom of God we, like Peter, have certain rights. According to John 20:22-23 when a repentant sinner stands before the altar on Sunday morning and repeats the prayer of salvation after me, I have the right to say, "Your sins are forgiven," and heaven will back me up. If a sinner refuses Christ and the work of Calvary, I likewise have the authority to say, "Your sins are retained." This is binding and loosing! Really, it has little to do with the casting out of demons. As far as the "binding of Satan" goes, for the most part, it is a religious exercise with little sanction or result.

The book of Revelation tells us that it will be a powerful angel who binds Satan for a thousand years and casts him into the bottomless pit. As one teacher remarked, the beginning of Satan's binding started the first time Jesus set someone free and will end in Revelation 20:2, which states,

> *He laid hold of the dragon, that serpent of old, who is the Devil and Satan, and bound him for a thousand years.*

You and I do not have the absolute authority to bind Satan permanently, but we surely help expedite his ultimate binding by setting people free from his hold. He is still the "god of this world," and let's not get into foolishness by thinking we can run around confessing, "I bind you, Satan, and that's that." Jesus demonstrated that the only thing that works is the spoken, revealed Word of God on the lips of a believer. "Satan, it is written..."

That will always stop him and his kind long enough for you and me to get the truth of the Bible into a person's soul. But just as in Jesus' case on the Mount of Temptation, Satan only leaves for a season. One thing you can say about our enemy is that he's tenacious, he doesn't quit!

It is lawful for you and me to put the Word of God in our hearts and in our mouths and boldly proclaim to the kingdom of darkness who we are in Christ:

> *Shall the prey be taken from the mighty, or the captives of the righteous be delivered? But thus says the Lord: "Even the*

captives of the mighty shall be taken away, and the prey of the terrible be delivered; for I will contend with him who contends with you, and I will save your children" (Is. 49:24-25).

And if Satan has risen up against himself, and is divided, he cannot stand, but has an end. No one can enter a strong man's house and plunder his goods, unless he first binds the strong man, and then he will plunder his house (Mk. 3:26-27).

The picture here is plain and simple, survival of the strongest. There are two schools of interpretation. The traditional exegesis is that Satan or the strong man is a demon, versus one stronger, i.e., Jesus, Paul, you and I, who can overpower him, bind him and chase him off some poor soul in need. I have no problem with that interpretation, but here is another angle to consider. Man, created in the image and likeness of God, was created both beautiful and powerful.

What is man that You are mindful of him, and the son of man that You visit him? For You have made him a little lower than the angels (God), and You have crowned him with glory and honor. You have made him to have dominion over the works of Your hands; You have put all things under his feet (Ps. 8:4-6).

Man fell into sin and his power was usurped by Satan. However, man, even in his fallen condition, was still very strong, as Genesis reveals,

But the Lord came down to see the city and the tower which the sons of men had built. And the Lord said, "Indeed the people are one and they all have one language, and this is what they begin to do; now nothing that they propose to do will be withheld from them" (Gen. 11:5-6).

Satan had power over man, for all had become "children of disobedience." We could say that Satan entered the strong man's house as a thief and plundered his goods because man was bound up with sin. But then, after Pentecost, a new species of beings were turned loose on this planet — Christians! Stronger than any devil, demon or unclean spirit, we Christians are taking back people and cities for God.

Wage the Good Warfare

This charge I commit to you, son Timothy, according to the prophecies previously made concerning you, that by them you may wage the good warfare (1 Tim. 1:18).

As General Patton once said, "You don't win a war by dying for your country. You win a war by making the other guy die for his country." A good war is one which we not only win, but one after which we're still around to enjoy the spoils of battle. Spiritual warfare can quickly wear a saint out unless he or she is constantly reminded that from Genesis to Revelation God has proclaimed and procured the victory.

And I will put enmity between you and the woman, and between your seed and her Seed; he shall bruise your head, and you shall bruise His heel (Gen. 3:15).

These will make war with the Lamb, and the Lamb will over come them, for He is Lord of lords and King of kings; and those who are with Him are called, chosen, and faithful (Rev. 17:14).

The rules and articles of war and how to win are seen in almost every book of the Bible, if one looks for them. Paul told his young protege Timothy,

You therefore must endure hardship as a good soldier of Jesus Christ. No one engaged in warfare entangles himself with the affairs of this life, that he may please him who enlisted him as a soldier. And also if anyone competes in athletics, he is not crowned unless he competes according to the rules (2 Tim. 2:3-5).

No one promised we wouldn't get shot at or even hit now and then, but to paraphrase Paul, "You can knock me down but you can't knock me out." Paul called the attacks of Satan, "light afflictions." What a blow to the warped ego of the prince of the power of the air!

All wars are violent. Jesus told us, "The kingdom of heaven suffers violence, and the violent take it by force" (Mt. 11:12). Our church services, music, prayer meetings, preaching, giving, witnessing, need a good old-fashioned dose of Holy Ghost violence. One of my closest friends often says, "If you're going to be a bear, be a grizzly." There are too many cute teddy bears filling our pews! Remember the uniform of the saint is not just a woolen garment, but armor, full armor!

No Pat Formulas!

Since my first book on warfare and the purging of the heavenlies was released, I have been inundated with requests for sample prayers. A group of Baptists from up north were all stirred up, but their first question was, "Do we have to speak in tongues to get in on this?" Just about every camp out there, including "born again" Catholic priests, get fired up over all this, but they all have questions: "Do we ask God to remove them?" "Are we to speak in our known tongue or simply intercede in the Spirit?" "What exactly do we say to the principalities anyway?"

These are just a sample of the questions from hungry souls craving direction and instruction. I certainly don't have all the answers, but I do know what works. We must always start from a position of strength, just as the Lord encouraged Joshua:

> Only be strong and very courageous, that you may observe to do according to all the law which Moses My servant commanded you; do not turn from it to the right hand or to the left, that you may prosper wherever you go. This book of the Law shall not depart from your mouth, but you shall meditate on it day and night, that you may observe to do according to all that is written in it. For then you will make your way prosperous, and then you will have good success (Josh. 1:7, 8).

Strength, courage, obedience and meditation on the Word of God is essential at the outset. Prayer, be it with one's intellect or in the Spirit, is like warming up before the big match. Don't be so quick to get into petitioning the Father with your "want list," but

101

learn from our forefathers. Praise Him first! Brag on His past exploits like King Jehoshaphat did in 2 Chronicles 20:5-11:

> Then Jehoshaphat stood in the congregation of Judah and Jerusalem, in the house of the Lord, before the new court, and said: "O Lord God of our fathers, are You not God in heaven, and do You not rule over all the kingdoms of the nations, and in Your hand is there not power and might, so that no one is able to withstand You? Are You not our God, who drove out the inhabitants of this land before Your people Israel, and gave it to the descendants of Abraham Your friend forever? And they dwell in it, and have built You a sanctuary in it for Your name, saying, 'If disaster comes upon us, such as the sword, judgment, pestilence, or famine, we will stand before this temple and in Your presence (for Your name is in this temple), and cry out to You in our affliction, and You will hear and save.' And now, here are the people of Ammon, Moab, and Mount Seir — whom You would not let Israel invade when they came out of the land of Egypt, but they turned from them and did not destroy them — here they are, rewarding us by coming to throw us out of Your possession which You have given us to inherit."

Notice, before the stressed-out monarch asked for God to intervene, he first reminded the Lord of past victories. We should always thank Him for saving us, healing us, blessing us with substance, and for all the wonderful things our God has done for us in the past before we hit the panic button over our present situation.

For those who are baptized in the Holy Ghost, Jude verse 20 exhorts: "But you, beloved, building yourselves up on your most holy faith, praying in the Holy Spirit..." Once again, these are all preparatory. You don't remove a powerful prince by talking to him in tongues!

> For he who speaks in a tongue does not speak to men but to God, for no one understands him; however, in the spirit he speaks mysteries. But he who prophecies speaks edification and exhortation and comfort to men. He who speaks in a

*tongue edifies himself, but he who prophesies edifies the
church. I wish you all spoke with tongues, but even more that
you prophesied; for he who prophesies is greater than he who
speaks with tongues, unless indeed he interprets, that the
church may receive edification* (1 Cor. 14:2-5).

Tongues, even in intercession (Rom. 8:26), is between your
spirit and God. It is a mystery, Paul says. No one, including a
demon, understands you (1 Cor. 14:2).

I was in Mexico awhile back and a policeman rattled off
something to me in Spanish. He had the badge and weapons of
one in authority, but I couldn't obey him because I couldn't
understand him. I finally figured out that my van was in the
wrong place.

To get the attention of the ruling evil spirits, all the way down
to the lowest of demons, you simply say what God has already
said. That worked for Jesus in Matthew 4, and it will work for
you. You must believe with all your heart that the Bible is
absolute authority. The Word coming out of your mouth has to
be "rhema," Holy Ghost anointed and full of power.

A good place to start is with Colossians 2:15:

*Having disarmed principalities and powers, He made a
public spectacle of them, triumphing over them in it.*

As one preacher said, "When Satan brings up your past, you
bring up his future." Speak directly to the spirit. Take the offen-
sive. Don't get into theological debates. Religious devils are
clever. Always mention the blood of Jesus. It torments them to
no end.

When Dr. Lester Sumrall was in Manila in 1953 and heard
the screams of a young demon-possessed prostitute over the
radio, he came to the rescue. The two demons cursed the blood
of Jesus out of fear, as if the blood had life of its own. To them the
blood and Jesus were one and the same.

As I mentioned previously, revival broke out over this one
deliverance. In addition to the spiritual keys of the Word there
are human keys in our cities. Sometimes one salvation, one

miracle, one healing, one word of knowledge or wisdom will unlock a whole region. Because of Lot, Abram (Abraham) stood in the gap. Rahab, the harlot, was very instrumental in taking Jericho. A Samaritan woman at the well went and told the whole city about a man who knew all about her. A demon-possessed sorceress was delivered by Paul and Silas, and a great church was birthed at Philippi. I believe that your city and mine have these key people waiting to be unlocked and that through their release, the flood of blessing will pour into our streets. How do we know who they are? We don't! Only God does and in His good time He will reveal them to us.

The last decade of this last century of this sixth millennium is destined to be the decade of warfare. We've seen various great moves of God in this twentieth century but the final conflict is upon us. Faith, prayer, the manifestation of the gifts, evangelism, intercession — all point to the nineties as a climactic period, reminiscent of Isaiah:

> *The Spirit of the Lord God is upon Me, because the Lord has anointed Me to preach good tidings to the poor; He has sent Me to heal the brokenhearted, to proclaim liberty to the captives, and the opening of the prison to those who are bound; to proclaim the acceptable year of the Lord, and the day of vengeance of our God; to comfort all who mourn, to console those who mourn in Zion, to give them beauty for ashes, the oil of joy for mourning, the garment of praise for the spirit of heaviness; that they may be called trees of righteousness, the planting of the Lord, that He may be glorified.*
>
> *And they shall rebuild the old ruins, they shall raise up the former desolations, and they shall repair the ruined cities, the desolations of many generations. Strangers shall stand and feed your flocks, and the sons of the foreigner shall be your plowmen and your vinedressers. But you shall be named the Priests of the Lord, men shall call you the Servants of our God. You shall eat the riches of the Gentiles, and in their glory*

you shall boast. Instead of your shame you shall have double honor, and instead of confusion they shall rejoice in their portion. Therefore in their land they shall possess double; everlasting joy shall be theirs (Is. 61:1-7).

CHAPTER 15

The Battle is the Lord's!

Who is like you, O Lord, among the gods? Who is like You, glorious in holiness, fearful in praises, doing wonders? (Ex. 15:11)

The Bible was inspired by God and written by men from the East. It is flavored with Eastern idioms. Being from the East, Orientals can more readily relate to the overall expression of God's Word. Here in the West, individuality is promoted; whereas in the Bible the emphasis is on the tribe, the nation or the body of Christ. The family clan or colony of people living together, praying together, working together is clearly understood by the Eastern mind. Shutting an old person away from the family was and still is unheard of in the Orient. Elders are reverenced and given great honor for their wisdom. Orientals are submissive by nature and understand authority. They favor doing things together as a unit.

Being a board member on Dr. Paul Cho's Church Growth International, I annually visit Korea to study the revival going on there. The Korean mind is very close to the Hebrew way of thinking. Many ask the question, "How can one man control 700,000 members?" The answer is simple. His congregation understands the Bible. Unlike many Americans who try to make the Bible a Western self-help guide to success and better living, Koreans believe it to be the voice and will of God. When their pastor speaks, it is the will of God and they obey. If he calls a collective fast, they fast. Here in America we feel it is our sovereign right to question, judge, criticize and leave our church if the pastor isn't saying what we believe. One of the most common phrases heard in American church circles is, "Well, I think..."

Greek Influences

The root of our rebellion can be traced to the influence the Greeks have had on our country. Dr. C. M. Ward, Dr. S. K. Sung and Dr. Lester Sumrall were over for lunch recently, and we all sat around discussing the impact of Greek ideology on the modern church. The Hebrews have no problem with God. They all pretty much have the same viewpoint of Jehovah. Jesus is, of course, a different story, but God is God Almighty.

Our American educational system is a by-product of the ancient Greeks. Consider their gods for a moment. They looked, even acted, like men except they had more power. The Greeks wanted their gods to be like them. How convenient! All false religions start with man and then work up to God. The Bible starts with God and works down to man.

Why is it that we have so many versions of God, His will, His power? We invite the unsaved to become Christians, and they answer, "Which kind?" What a choice! There's Baptist, Methodist, Presbyterian, Lutheran, Pentecostal, Charismatic, Word of Faith, Kingdom Now, Assembly of God, Foursquare, and the list continues to grow. We all claim to have the market on truth. We fight over it, preach against others, even hint that they may not even be saved. Some present a god who's a real nice guy — you know, "Once saved, always saved" no matter what. On the other end of the gospel spectrum, we have a God who takes away the new birth every time one sins — a cranky, touchy Lord. Some have a God you can only contact through a priest. Others have One who hates color, music, modern fashion and television — kind of a stodgy old fuddy-duddy. Then some present a retired God who is out of the miracle, healing, delivering, tongues and prophecy business. Let's not leave out the funky, semi-hyper, shouting, dancing, tambourine-playing Lord who loves to get down all afternoon! The variations on the theme of God we Americans present is a long one, too long for one book.

We all create God in our own image. We all think He's just like us. This thinking has seeped in from Ancient Greek culture, and it's fatal! Listen to the dire warning in Psalms 50:21:

> *These things you have done, and I kept silent; You thought that I was altogether like you; But I will reprove you, and set them in order before your eyes.*

Let's let our God be God!

Teamwork is Essential

> *Or what king, going to make war against another king, does not sit down first and consider whether he is able...* (Lk. 14:31).

Our ability to make war against the government of Satan is extremely hindered by our selfish need for individuality. We have forgotten that our sole function is to glorify God and do His will.

> *You therefore must endure hardship as a good soldier of Jesus Christ. No one engaged in warfare entangles himself with the affairs of this life, that he may please Him who enlisted him as a soldier* (2 Tim. 2:3-4).

Perhaps we all need a closer look at Who it is that enlists us. The Lord of hosts is a Warrior-King, Man-of-War.

> *For behold, the Lord, the Lord of hosts, takes away from Jerusalem and from Judah the stock and the store, the whole supply of bread and the whole supply of water; the mighty man and the man of war* (Is. 3:1-2).

> *Then I saw heaven opened, and behold, a white horse. And He who sat on him was called Faithful and True, and in righteousness He judges and makes war. His eyes were like a flame of fire, and on His head were many crowns. He had a name written that no one knew except Himself. He was clothed with a robe dipped in blood, and His name is called The Word of God. And the armies in heaven, clothed in fine linen, white and clean, followed Him on white horses. Now*

out of His mouth goes a sharp sword, that with it He should strike the nations. And He Himself will rule them with a rod of iron. He Himself treads the winepress of the fierceness and wrath of Almighty God. And He has on His robe and on His thigh a name written: KING OF KINGS AND LORD OF LORDS (Rev. 19:11-16).

Many have reduced the Lord to their personal "little buddy," who is there to listen to their problems, smooth their ruffled feathers, and pat them on the head as if to say, "Oh, don't worry about it; I'll see to it; it's all okay." But we are to obey our Sovereign Supreme Commander and hide (treasure) His Word in our hearts:

Now acquaint yourself with Him, and be at peace; thereby good will come to you. Receive, please, instruction from His mouth, and lay up His words in your heart (Job 22:21-22).

In taking time to read and study the Bible, we should also allow the Bible to read and study us. As one writer commented, "You can't look into God's Word without God looking into you."

Our God is Incomparable!

Who is like You, O Lord, among the gods? Who is like You, glorious in holiness, fearful in praises, doing wonders? You stretched out Your right hand; the earth swallowed them. You in Your mercy have led forth the people whom You have redeemed; You have guided them in Your strength to Your holy habitation (Ex. 15:11-13).

God is at once both the Fountainhead and Foundation of all goodness, all truth, all righteousness.

Arthur W. Pink expresses it beautifully in one of his books (*Attributes of God*, Moody Press, pgs. 9 & 10):

In the beginning, God (Gen. 1:1). There was a time, if time it could be called, when God, in the unity of His nature (through subsisting equally in three Divine Persons), dwelt all alone. In the beginning, God. There was no heaven, whether His glory is now particularly manifested. There was no earth to engage His attention. There were no angels to hymn His praises; no universe to be upheld by the word of His power. There was nothing, no one, but God; and that, not for a day, a year, or an age, but from everlasting. During a past eternity, God was alone: self-contained, self-sufficient, self-satisfied; in need of nothing. Had a universe, had angels, had human beings been necessary to Him in any way, they also had been called into existence from all eternity. The creating of them when He did, added nothing to God essentially. He changes not (Mal. 3:6); therefore His essential glory can be neither augmented nor diminished.

God was under no constraint, no obligation, no necessity to create. That He chose to do so was purely a sovereign act on His part, caused by nothing outside Himself, determined by nothing but His own mere good pleasure; for He worketh all things after the counsel of His own will (Eph. 1:11). That He did create was simply for His manifestive glory. Do some of our readers imagine that we have gone beyond what Scripture warrants? Then our appeal shall be to the Law and the Testimony: "Stand up and bless the Lord your God forever and ever: and blessed be Thy glorious name, which is exalted above all blessing and praise" (Neh. 9:5). God is no gainer even from our worship. He was in no need of that external glory of His grace which arises from His redeemed, for He is glorious enough in Himself without that. What was it that moved Him to predestinate His elect to the praise of the glory of His grace? It was, as Ephesians 1:5 tells us, according to the good pleasure of His will.

The more all of us in the various streams of Christianity keep focused on our awesome Lord, our Source and Spring, the less we will look at each other with contempt. Once we start working and fighting together under the direction of the Captain of our salvation, the more we'll like one another, maybe even love one another!

"You're a dreamer, Bernal!" many will say. Well, it's amazing what happens when a nation comes under attack. No more

Democrats or Republicans, only Americans. If nothing else, we're going to have to unite to survive this next decade of destiny.

Win or Else!

What is the price to pay for engaging in warfare and not winning? All one has to do is look at the Vietnam fiasco. The streets of my city are filled with war-torn rejects who have no self respect. They were thrown into an unpopular campaign with very little support from the folks back home. We hear about the MIA's (Missing in Action), but what about the thousands of vets who are missing life's blessings because they lost. The frustration for many is overpowering.

In contrast, see how proud our veterans from World War II are! They won. The enemy was soundly defeated. Our country rallied behind the conflict. The battle lines were clearly defined.

One of the big problems in fighting idol worshippers is no one really knows what kind of demon activity went on in Vietnam. We know drug addiction, lawlessness and foxhole conversions with no real attempt to follow through, added to the problem. It is painfully obvious that many who roam our streets talking to themselves, or to a voice from an unseen entity, are demonized. Their only hope is total deliverance and restoration. As one coach said, "Winning isn't everything, it's the only thing."

A wise minister told me, "Once you declare war on the area principality you can't quit, call time out, or ease up. If you do, you'll have no rest, no peace. The evil spirit will make a mockery of your feeble effort. He'll torment you to no end."

It amazes me how people think backsliding is the way to get out from under pressure. The reality of it is that God doesn't take away our problems, He gives us the strength to overcome them! Leaving church or the ministry because of a mistake is wrong. You fight until you win. You keep in there until the Lord says the round is over. Satan isn't going to leave you alone simply because you have decided to go back into the world. It will be worse than before, much worse. Fight to win! Make each blow count for the Kingdom of God. There is no turning back!

CHAPTER 16

Testimony From Nebraska

Pastor Neal Hail from Scotts Bluff, Nebraska, called me one day to share this amazing story. Pastor Hail was a former executive officer with the 700 Club and a seasoned minister of the gospel. His church read my first book, *Storming Hell's Brazen Gates*, and it helped them to put more pieces of the puzzle together. They realized that the skies were shut over their community, and they longed for a breakthrough, just like Isaiah,

> *Oh that You would rend the heavens! That you would come down! That the mountains might shake at Your presence — As fire burns brushwood, as fire causes water to boil — to make Your name known to Your adversaries, that the nations may tremble at Your presence! (Is. 64:1-2)*

They had a plan of attack and it worked beautifully. Pastor Hail's wife, Janelle, sent the following report:

CHRISTIANS IN SCOTTSBLUFF DECLARE, "NO DROUGHT WILL COME NEAR OUR LAND!"

The Western Panhandle of Nebraska seats the twin cities of Scottsbluff/Gering, population 25,000. Geographically remote and forgotten by men, God has not forgotten this area. God has done an incredible miracle! In the midst of the drought-ridden and parched land of the United States, this oasis, described as a "Garden of Eden," has sprung up in this agricultural-based land. Recently, cattlemen from Montana have brought 22,000 head of cattle to graze on its fertile pasture land. Cattlemen and farm-related industry from as far as Canada have come to participate in its rich wheat harvest and luscious pastures. No drought exists in Western Nebraska!

For centuries this land has been held at ransom by the devil as dominant spiritual forces have covered the valley with spiritual darkness. Drought, disaster and tragedy have ruled and reigned over the valley. Pastor Neal Hail, Senior Pastor of First Assembly of God, Scottsbluff, Nebraska, for nearly two years says, "Through extensive preaching of the Word, much light has filled the valley with the knowledge of God."

Last April, in obedience to the Word of God, God's people began to pray 2 Chronicles 7:14, "If My people, which are called by My name, shall humble themselves, and pray, and seek My face, and turn from their wicked ways; then will I hear from heaven, and will forgive their sin, and will heal their land."

Pastors Neal and Janelle Hail led their congregation in a 40-day fast to seek God for the healing of their land. At the time the fast began, the land was cracked and dry. Planting season would soon be starting, and after a tragic storm last year, which destroyed crops, the livelihood of the valley would depend upon good crop yield in 1988.

A Spiritual Task Force was formed, consisting of 21 persons, who led the people in spiritual warfare against the devil. For three weeks, training sessions were held at the church to equip the Spiritual Task Force with a battle plan to pull down spiritual wickedness in high places that had dominated the valley and imprisoned its people.

The battle plan was basically this:

1) Identification of the enemy — They uncovered the tactics of Satan in their area. Library research and historical books of the area revealed the spirit in which the area was founded, and the Spirit of God revealed the dominant spirits that set up rulership over the territory.

116

2) Spiritual Reinforcement — They researched the Scriptures to unseat these spiritual forces, as identified to them by the Holy Spirit, and prayed the Word of God against the spirits of darkness.

3) Charging the Devil — "Flee, in Jesus' Name!" they cried. No power of darkness could stand against the name of Jesus! Satan had to flee and take his hierarchy of demons with him.

4) Establishment of God's Kingdom As The Ruling Force Over The Area — No longer would Satan rule, but God's people cleared the atmosphere of hindering demons who had stopped the flow of God's power and presence. Now, the way they lived would be based upon the Word, which brings healing and well-being to the land and the people.

On the fourth week, the Spiritual Task Force marched up a high bluff overlooking the valley, called Scottsbluff National Monument, which has been renamed "Victory Mountain" by the group. By force they stormed the gates of hell, demanding Satan to release their valley from bondage. The presence of God settled over that mountain as His people partook of communion, eating and drinking a portion, then scattering the remainder over the valley as an eternal monument to their God. As they sang praises to the Lord, the sound of the shofar burst forth a note of victory toward the heavenlies — OUR GOD REIGNS!

At the conclusion of the 40-day fast, in which the entire congregation had participated, there was a great rejoicing before the Lord in the feast and time of praise.

The result has been the mighty move of the Spirit of God over the valley. A beautiful, unseasonal, wet snowfall came in April, the beginning of perfectly timed moisture in accord with the planting season. May and June saw above-average rainfall. The parched land has turned into rolling green farmland, amazingly noticeable to the surrounding 60 mile radius of drought lands. A bountiful harvest of beans, wheat, and corn along with rich grazing land for the cattle now fills the valley. Only God could do such a mighty work! As the Spirit of the Lord told Pastor Hail, "Reward is yours, all glory is Mine!"

CHAPTER 17

Loving Your City

We fight for that which we love the most. At times, even with no regard to our personal safety, we will "lay down our lives" if need be. A parent sees his child in peril and moves with compassion to rescue the object of his affection. A friend of mine, who is really a poor swimmer, told me how a few years ago he and his family were camping up in the mountains near a lake. His youngest boy was way out past the diving raft and struggling to reach safety. My friend Curt dove in, clothes and all, and made his way quickly to his drowning son. After it was all over he couldn't believe he even attempted such a feat.

Love is as powerful as it is wonderful! We must love our cities. Jesus loved Jerusalem and wept over it. The Lord promised Abraham's seed would "possess the gates of their enemies" (Gen. 22:17). Our cities' gates need to be possessed by godly people. I have recently joined the San Jose Chamber of Commerce so I can rub elbows with the decision-makers of our city. It has already payed off. Our city fathers should never make a major decision without the counsel or the leading of a seasoned pastor's input.

Not long ago, I was in Seoul, Korea on church business. Dr. Cho, my elder Dr. Dennis Kim, and a leading Baptist minister from Texas were playing a round of golf. While we were on the 13th tee, a big black car pulled up nearby and an official-looking type started running toward us, speaking extremely rapidly in Korean. I could tell something important was up. I whispered to my elder, "Dennis, what's going on?" "Big time, pastor" he replied. "There is an emergency at parliament, and the president needs Dr. Cho to come." Now that's influence — not merely in a city but in a whole nation!

One of the reasons we Christians have such a hard time getting elected to office is our track record. We love preaching more than serving. People vote for servants who have been involved in the problems of their region. I was interviewing Colonel Doner, the author of *The Samaritan Strategy*, not long ago on television and he brought out a very interesting point. Why is Mother Teresa so widely received and a well-known evangelical almost scorned? She has a record of service to dying humanity. Her doctrine and knowledge of the Bible may not be perfect or scholarly, but she loves and she serves.

Jesus said, "Let your light shine." We would rather be heard. A preacher of righteousness must also be a "doer of righteousness."

A young minister from Yakima, Washington, sent me his thoughts on the subject of possessing our cities. Pastor David Shirk made some very interesting notes which I'll pass along to you.

> *A great need in this hour is for church leaders to begin cultivating relationships within their communities with other spiritual leadership for the purpose of waiting upon God for the strategy, the empowering and the winning of their cities. It requires a willful decision to see this as God's priority. When Solomon began to do in the natural what the church is called to do in the spiritual, i.e. build a house for the name of the Lord, he did it this way. 1) Now Solomon **decided** to build a house for the name of the Lord, (2 Chron. 2:1). 2) **Then** Solomon **began** to build the house for the Lord, (3:1). 3) Thus Solomon **finished** the house of the Lord" (5:1). Without a decision there will be no beginning. Without a beginning there will be no finishing.*

> *For several years now in my own city of Yakima, Washington, God has stirred my heart to join myself with the other leaders of this community of 100,000+ to discern His will for*

our city. I have been inspired by men who have seen the call to win their cities as the primary reason for their placement in the locale. These men are modeling something for leaders everywhere.

As a theological framework for the idea of winning a city, of possessing the gates of an enemy, we have the story of Abraham and Isaac in Genesis 22. In verse 17 God promises "your seed shall possess the gates of their enemies." He goes on to say it is because of obedience. In all the covenant promises that God made to Abraham previously (ch. 12, 15 and 17), He had never promised the "gates" of the enemy cities to Abraham's seed. What was there about that hot lonely day on Mt. Moriah that initiated this covenant promise from God.

Chapter 22 is filled with many types and applications. It is the first place where two key Scriptural words find their expression. It is the first place where the word 'love' appears in the Bible. It is also the first place where the word 'worship' appears. God is declaring that the great triangle of His purpose is to be seen in this story of obedience being at the heart of love, and love being at the heart of worship. Obedience, love and worship all play an important part in the salvation of a city.

The promise of possessing the gates of enemy cities is released through the type of Isaac as the chosen Son. Isaac was obedient to the point of death. Abraham is a type of the Father, who spared not his only son (v. 16). When this type was fulfilled it released the anointing of "possessing the gates." This anointing to break the enemy's back in the place of his own stronghold was given to us through Jesus as the obedient Son, given by the willing Father, to win the world. When the church fulfills her place as the people of God, fully obedient to the authority of God, we will carry this 'back-breaking' authority to win our cities. We will begin to see the "rod of iron" and the "rule of God" (Ps. 2) extended over our communities.

Jesus, as the descendant son of Abraham, advances this anointing to the chosen "seed," the church, in Matthew 16:18. Jesus said, "I will build My church; and the gates of Hades shall not overpower it." If you read through the story of Ruth and other Old Testament accounts, you will see that gates refer to the place of "civil authority" in a city. It amounts to a current day 'city hall.' A police officer has authority in your city because he represents City Hall. When Jesus promises that Hades' gates shall not prevail, what is He saying?

The traditional interpretation is that God here promises the church the ability to "hold the fort" against the devil's onslaught. In reality the opposite is the meaning. Jesus promises that the devil won't be able to "hold his fort" against the onslaught of the church. The place of the devil's authority, the 'city hall' of hell, the fountain of all that is impure and evil in your community, God promises will not, in fact cannot, resist a people of the chosen seed, who are willing to go in "violently and take it by force." The church has been tricked in the past. Tricked into thinking that we had to 'defend' something that never really needed defending. If we are defending we cannot at the same time be offending. God has called us to offend hell. To hold captive what Jesus has taken captive from that "city of darkness."

Unfortunately we too often in our cities have given up rule of God's power and find ourselves now having to take back our relinquished cities from the jaws of Satan's power (Rev. 2:13). Jesus came back from the grave with the "keys of death and Hades." If we can see that Jesus, as the fulfillment of Isaac, Himself possessed the gates of the greatest enemy of all; the city below the earth (Eph. 4:9), shouldn't the church see herself anointed to continue this ruination of darkness, by winning the cities above the earth?

In the process of winning our city of Yakima, I am observing at least six strategies that God provides to possess a city. I believe these principles apply to any city, and, in time, can be collectively discerned through the prayer and counsel of Christian leaders in a community.

1. Discern the gate(s) of your city, identify who has control of them, and commit yourselves to prayer.

Then Moses stood in the gate of the camp, and said, "Whoever is for the Lord, come to me!" (Ex. 32:26). In this account of Moses' anger being kindled because of the golden calf, we see this first principle in motion. Moses really knew how to cleanse sin from the camp! To do the work of cleansing this 'nomadic city' he took his place of responsibility to "stand in the gates." When people of spiritual anointing responsibly fulfill their call, they have this same anointing to cleanse a city.

Gates are nothing more than access points to the entrance of a city. Part of Solomon's anointing was that he knew how, "to go in and out before the people" (1 Kings 3:7). There was a reason why God called the elders to "sit in the gates," rather than to transact their business in some cloistered, smoke-filled room up in the ivory tower. Men and women of anointing need to be where the action is. The action is in the gates.

Sin brings exposure. Consider Adam and Eve, "Lord, I was naked" (Gen. 3:10). Spiritual coverings are given to diminish the effect of exposure. In the garden, it was because of sin that the first coverings were made (Gen. 3:21). They were made by God Himself. When we truly sit in the gates and possess them, no matter what the area of responsibility is, whether it be as a political leader, an employer, a father or mother, a teacher or a pastor, we are given the empowerment from God to extend spiritual coverings, to lessen the effects of exposure to sin. This was the anointing Moses had on that fateful first Pentecost evening. On the first Pentecost under the law 3,000 died. Praise God that on the first Pentecost of the Spirit 3,000 were made alive.

God is calling the church of this and other nations to identify the access points of their cities. What are the places of influence that shape and mold the life and death of your city? Are they to be found in key political offices, in the minds of certain city planners or entrepreneurial developers? Is it certain financiers that have control of the gates? **Dallas' J. R.** Ewing graphically portrays the picture of not just a man but a spiritual force (not for good) that sits in one of the gates of a city, and influences its destiny. All across the land God is raising up Christians who have the burden to face the public through the media and run for political office. Some of these people will have the opportunity to possess a gate for God in their city. They can be empowered to extend God's covering to bless that city. We must pray for men and women of God who righteously control an access point.

As we pray, God gives us discernment to know where the gates are, and who it is that is occupying them. Maybe it's the porn hustlers, the union bosses, the drug dealers or organized crime heads, or false religious leaders. Once we see, we become equipped to war effectively. Remember the Lord told Joshua, "see, I have given Jericho into your hands" (Josh. 6:2). We are no longer "ignorant of the enemy's devices."

It is through the gates that the enemy "comes into your city like a flood," it is through prayer and anointed warfare that God releases us to storm those gates, to open up heaven to "Jacob's ladder" and the help of the heavenly hosts, and to be the standard that God raises up to make your city a city of refuge and righteousness. Be a catalyst in your community! Gather some of the 'elders of your city' and begin to share and pray and see if the Spirit does not begin to show you "what eye hath not seen."

2. Understand the heritage of your city.

"And He gave their land as a heritage, a heritage to Israel His people" (Ps. 135:12). A city always has a heritage. For Israel, it was the heathen heritage of some of the cities that they dispossessed that in future years came back to haunt them. They often allowed the godlessness of those people to dilute and divert their spiritual energies away from the one true God.

Understanding the history and the heritage of your city will give you a deep insight into the present-day structure that *is shaping it. Consider answering some of these questions: Why was this city settled? Who were the kinds of people instrumental in its founding? What was their motive for settlement? What key events have shaped its history?*

Let me give some examples of how powerful this knowledge can be in determining the current spiritual forces at work in a community. Consider Los Angeles and the Hollywood mentality. Much of the reason for the settling of the great state of California was to accommodate the rampant greed of the California gold rush. Today materialism is still at the root of identity of many of its key cities. Consider the great effects of Ellis Island and the rush of immigrants that today affect life in New York City. Consider the effects of the civil war and the burning of Atlanta that have shaped the life of that great southern city. How about the history of the river boat queen and New Orleans? Does the mentality of a hard-working ethic in a steel mill town like Pittsburgh give rise to a works/ righteousness mentality in spiritual things?

I remember being on a tour of the "underground" Seattle, a series of caverns that once contained a great alternative to merchant life directly above. The tour guide suggested that the reason for the establishment of this part of the city was to competitively 'undercut' the businesses above. How does that conniving spirit of competition affect spiritual unity in that city today?

Understanding the history of what has already 'flooded through the gates' of your city will give some clear indications as to what 'strong men' now are needing to be bound and plundered. In the winning of your city, knowing these points of spiritual disobedience to God is helpful. We will probably never know them all, yet we need to allow God the opportunity to show us. Many of the kings of the Old Testament had to take their nation back to the point of disobedience and build from that place in faith, to again see God's favor.

3. Know the covenants that have been made.

"Nevertheless, I will remember My covenant with you in the days of your youth" (Ezek. 16:60). *In this chapter God is comparing the different fates of certain sister cities; Sodom, Samaria, Jerusalem. He declares that the destiny of these cities and their eventual salvation or destruction is, at least in part, dictated by God's past covenants with them. Could Lot have saved Sodom by "spiritually" sitting in the gates of that city before it was totally reprobated? God told Abraham He would save Sodom if Lot could show even a minuscule percentage of righteousness in its people. Could that homosexual spirit that brought on destruction have been bound the year before?*

Do you ever wonder what covenants with darkness have been made in certain places by people entrusted to lead their cities? How about Salem, Massachusetts? Or San Francisco? Or New Orleans? Or Las Vegas?

Breaking the covenants of old was an important part of Israel's dispossession of enemy lands. It was also an important part of the New Testament church. Paul asked, "What covenant hath light with darkness?" (2 Cor. 6:14). *Many cities live under a cloak of darkness that the church much penetrate with covenant-breaking deliverance.*

What are the covenants with God that have been made by key people in your city? Many of our western and northwestern cities were founded with the heart to spread the gospel of Jesus Christ. Missionaries braving the elements, endangered on every front to spread the good news. I believe that God remembers these foundations.

I researched in our public library the history of the beginnings of Yakima. In that research I discovered what it was that brought the missionaries to Central Washington. The Indian nations had a great conclave in the Yakima river basin to talk about the favor of the great spirit upon the Lewis and Clark expedition. Why were they not annihilated by other Indian tribes? They had heard that these men believed in

God, and this God could be discovered in a great Book of Heaven. The Chieftain's Counsel had heard that this book could be found in St. Louis. They sent four of their strongest braves to bring back this Book of Heaven. Upon arrival in St. Louis one brave was killed immediately, a second not long afterward. After several weeks of fruitless searching for this Book of Heaven, the other two braves, totally disheartened, prepared to leave. The following words were recorded as these two braves shared their heart with the Secretary of Indian Affairs, General William Clark, the same man who had explored their land years before.

"We came to you, over a trail of many moons, from the setting sun. You were the friend of our fathers, who all have gone the long way. We came with our eyes partly opened for more light for our people who sit in darkness. We go back with our eyes closed. How can we go back, blind, to our blind people? We made our way to you with strong arms, through enemies and strange lands, that we might carry back much to them. We go back with arms broken and empty. The fathers who came with us, the braves of many winters and wars, we leave here asleep by your great water and wigwam. They were tired with their journey and their moccasins were worn out. Our people sent us to get the white man's Book of Heaven. You took us where they worship the Great Spirit with candles, but the Book was not there. You showed us images of good spirits, and pictures of a good land beyond, but the Book is not among them. We are going back the long, sad trail to our people. When we tell them, after one more snow, in the big council that we did not bring the Book, no word will be spoken by our old men nor by our young braves. One by one they will rise up and go out in silence. Our people will die in darkness, and they will go on the long path to the other hunting grounds. No white man will go with them and no Book of Heaven will make the way plain. We have no more words."

These words, recorded by Clark's clerk, circulated throughout newspapers across the Northeast. They inspired and spawned a great missionary outpouring for these hungry people who sat in darkness. Covenants were made with God, as missionary after missionary set out for the desolate lands of the West. I believe that God is remembering these covenants today. The great leaders of the Scriptures all knew how to do one thing well, remind God of His former covenants!

4. Use the Keys.

"I will give you the keys to the kingdom of heaven; and whatever you shall bind on earth shall have been bound in heaven, and whatever you shall loose on earth shall have been loosed in heaven" (Mt. 16:19).

Jesus is giving here, some of the structure of this 'back-breaking' anointing that He conveys to possess the gates of a city. He portrays that there are certain 'keys' to accomplish this work. These Greek perfect passive participles, "...shall have been bound," and "shall have been loosed," convey with great strength the completion and finished aspect of this anointing to bind and loose.

Using the keys is equal to spiritual warfare. It is the actual going out and dispossessing others from the gates. The powers of binding and loosing in intercession, in witness, in song, in confession and in prophetic command cannot be underestimated. When you have discerned that there is an enemy in a certain gate of your city, go to that gate (whether in spirit or in flesh) and speak to it with keys of the Kingdom. You may have to speak to the porn shop, or the prostitution capital or to the city government and say, "In the name of Jesus I command this gate to give way; I command it to give up its dead." Isaiah prophesied with the keys in his mouth, saying "say to the north, Give them up! And say to the south 'Do not hold them back'" (Is. 43:6). God is going to give you great courage as you begin to speak to the gates of your city as Joshua did to Jericho.

The keys are also the actual strategies for penetrating and winning your city. Strategies of outreach and evangelization, concerts of prayer, unified efforts of opposition, etc. We must be ready to move in obedience to the practical strategies that God unfolds for our communities.

There are five New Testament keys: the keys of the kingdom of God (Mt. 16:9); the key of knowledge (Lk. 11:52); the keys of death and Hades (Rev. 1:18); the key of the bottomless pit (Rev. 9:1, 20:1); and the key of David (Rev. 3:7).

Five keys and hallelujah, Jesus owns them all! Much could be said about the importance of each one of these in winning a city; however, for brevity sake simply remember: If you have the keys, you have access to the house. Let God open your eyes to see the function of these keys in the winning of your city.

5. Discern the prophetic role and calling of your city.

"And the cities that you shall give... shall be cities of refuge" (Num. 35:6). Discerning your city's prophetic calling is not easy. It must be addressed with great gentleness and humble submissiveness to others in the Body of Christ. In many ways, a person's discernment is only just that — one man's opinion. Listen to the common voice of the Spirit in the leadership of your community. Is God putting something consistent in your hearts? We know we are close when we hear, "the Spirit and the Bride say..."

A number of spiritual leaders in Los Angeles are aware of the great influence that that city has on world view. As the originator of so much in the music and film industries, they are aware of the prophetic call upon their city to be a clarion voice of communication for God to the four corners of our urban planet.

A cautionary word is in order. God is not interested in polarizing our cities. He does not want all the intellectuals in one city or the communicators in another or the musicians in *yet another. The church in a city is leaven. God wants to leaven the whole lump, not just particular stratas of our cities. The whole church is called to the whole community. I do believe, however, we will see certain role distinctions begin to take place in our cities as they yield to God's unfolding plan for this nation.*

6. Worship.

Before a city can be saved, the church must first be saved. Possessing the gates of your city is a plea for our cities to be awakened unto righteousness. It must first, however, become the experience of the Body of Christ. Paul said that God would be "quick to punish all disobedience, as soon as our (the church) obedience is complete" (2 Cor. 10:6). Worship is one of the great "keys" for this to happen. We are going to see in the years ahead a ground swell of worship rise so high that only the earth-quaking coming of Jesus will satisfy it. Worship is going to play an essential role in equipping the church to win our cities.

The Greek word translated 'worship' is 'proskuneo.' The word literally means "to kiss."

The parallels between the current state of the Body of Christ and the old fairy tale of Sleeping Beauty are almost extraordinary. Remember how the woman in her youthful years of beauty and innocence was deceived by the serpent witch to take a bite of the poisonous apple. Her deception led her into a great slumber. She did not grow less beautiful. She did not lose her rightful place. She did not die. She merely slept. One day an heir apparently appeared. A soon-coming King happened upon this sleeping girl, and He "desired her beauty." It was only His kiss that was required to bring her out of her slumber. She then wed herself to her Bridegroom, and they lived in their new kingdom happily ever after.

The "kiss of worship" will bring us, His bride, to full awakening. It will cause us to join ourselves wholly to Jesus. For, "like a chaste virgin, we have been betrothed unto one husband, even Christ" (2 Cor. 11:2).

Let us give ourselves to worshipping the King, and see as Jehoshaphat, that "when they began singing and praising, the Lord set ambushes against their enemies, and so they were routed" (2 Chron. 20:22). Let us open our hearts and mouths wide in worship and praise and "Shout! For the Lord hath given us the city."

CHAPTER 18

A Final Thought

I have made the earth, and created man on it. It was I — my hands that stretched out the heavens, and all their host I have commanded. I have raised him up in righteousness, and I will direct all his ways; He shall build My city and let My exiles go free, not for price nor reward, Says the Lord of hosts (Is. 45:12-13).

Then they cried out to the Lord in their trouble, and He delivered them out of their distresses. And He led them forth by the right way, that they might go to a city for habitation. Oh, that men would give thanks to the Lord for His goodness, and for His wonderful works to the children of men! (Ps. 107:6-8)

To reiterate once again, we must fall in love with our city. Like a father who sees his precious child in peril and casts caution to the wind and with compassion saves his beloved. Do you love your city? Are you willing to lay down your life for it? Will someone out there pay the price?

...then I said, Here am I! Send me (Is. 6:8).

Proclamation

Hear us, O spirits of darkness! We, the people of God, anointed by the Holy Spirit to preach the Gospel to the poor, to heal the brokenhearted, to proclaim liberty to the captives and to set free those who are bound and oppressed, and to proclaim the acceptable year of the Lord, stand fast and strong and courageous in our calling. We remind you, principalities and powers, that the Scriptures also say that the works that Jesus did, we who believe will do also, and even greater works. Our Lord's early disciples declared, "Lord, even the demons are subject to us in Your Name." We, too, have been given authority to trample on serpents and scorpions, and over all the power of the enemy, and nothing by any means shall hurt us.

Listen to us, spirits of arrogance, haughtiness, contention, religion, perversion, mammon, addiction, sorcery, murder, war, fear, anger, greed, death, poverty, infirmity and deception. We command you to come down from your high places! Our Father God has promised us in His holy Word that we will "possess the gates of our enemies."

Your rule and dominion shall be no more! All things were made through Jesus, and without Him nothing was made that was made. In Him was life, and this life was the light of men, and the light shines in the darkness and the darkness did not comprehend, nor overcome it. You are powerless to stop an awakening of righteousness in the hearts of men, women and children in our cities. We, the children of light, washed clean by the blood of the Lamb, penetrate your strongholds of evil. What Joshua said to the children of Israel upon approaching Jericho, we now declare and proclaim as the army of God, "Shout, for the Lord has given us the city!"

About the Cover

San Francisco is one of the most recognizable cities on the planet, with its unique skyline, picturesque hills, and, of course, its Golden Gate Bridge. This small, but world-class city (population 720,000) exerts an immeasurable influence upon Western culture. From the wild days of the Barbary Coast, almost any behavior or belief was acceptable in San Francisco. The Bay Area has always attracted the brilliant, liberal, ambitious, unsatisfied and bizarre.

More than anyone fully realizes, San Francisco exports ideas: the Beatnik Poets of the fifties led the way for the hippie counterculture, the anti-war and free-speech movement, the sexual revolution, gay liberation and the New Age cults. The Hedonism of the sixties has given way to the neo-paganism that is rampant today. No doubt today's blatant paganism has been influenced by Asian idolatry and mysticism.

This gateway city is a port of entry for alien ideas and alien forces. The devil has built a stronghold in San Francisco. He builds his citadels in beautiful cities like San Francisco. For one hundred and forty years Satan has had an open door into San Francisco, a hellish gate through which demons can pass to unwary America. We, through prayer, are pulling this and other strongholds down where hitherto the rulers of darkness have prevailed. When revival comes to San Francisco, and it will, the reverberations of our spiritual victory will shake the dark powers throughout America.

Christian, this is a call to arms! America is in a state of siege. From now until Jesus returns, we will be increasingly occupied by all-out spiritual warfare.